Burton, Mrs Harrison

An edelweiss of the Sierras

Golden-rod, and other tales

Burton, Mrs Harrison

An edelweiss of the Sierras
Golden-rod, and other tales

ISBN/EAN: 9783743313026

Manufactured in Europe, USA, Canada, Australia, Japa

Cover: Foto ©ninafisch / pixelio.de

Manufactured and distributed by brebook publishing software (www.brebook.com)

Burton, Mrs Harrison

An edelweiss of the Sierras

CONTENTS

	PAGE
AN EDELWEISS OF THE SIERRAS	3
GOLDEN-ROD: AN IDYL OF MOUNT DESERT	27
UNDER THE CONVENT WALL	135
CHERRYCOTE	147
THE SHATTERED VIOLIN	163
A HOUSE BUILT UPON THE SAND	173
ON A HILL-TOP	197

AN EDELWEISS OF THE SIERRAS

I

Lucy Boynton lived a solitary life in a gray old minster town in England. She was an orphan, in charge of a venerable maiden aunt who, like the celebrated "Mrs. F." of Hood's ballad, was

> "so very deaf
> She might have worn a percussion-cap,
> And be hit on the head without hearing it snap."

From spring to autumn, from autumn to spring, Lucy sat and sewed, dusted the tea-cups on the mantel-shelf, read a few dull books, and accompanied her aunt to service whence the morning and evening chants floated in at the window of their sitting-room close to the cathedral walls. Not so much as the Vicar of Wakefield's excitement "to migrate from the blue bed to the brown" was allotted her; for ever since she could remember, Lucy had occupied the same still, white-curtained nest, opening from Miss Boynton's bedroom, where at night she could peep out to supervise the removal of a certain glossy, ink-black frontispiece of hair, and the assumption of a frilled coif, converting the old lady's strong aquiline profile into a grim silhouette of some warrior of ancient Greece or Rome.

Into this colorless existence, when Lucy was about eighteen, there came an influence potent and mysterious, as if a waft of jasmine scent were blown across some meadow nook where homely buttercups are springing in the grass.

Miss Boynton's nephew, Tom Boynton, of whom his few scattered kinspeople had heard nothing for several years, arrived from the other side of the Atlantic to look up those of his blood remaining to him in England. He was a handsome, active young fellow, with a jaunty grace of carriage and a *timbre* in his hearty voice, irresistibly compelling a return of cordiality, be the recipient never so guarded in his dignity.

Innocent Lucy, herself perhaps not quite up to the standard of dignity at St. Margaret's in general, fell in love with him frankly at the outset, while Tom, who began by finding no end of pleasure in telling his traveller's tales to this dear little wide-eyed creature, growing white and red alternately with his perils and escapes, ended by picking her up in his arms one day, and vowing he must have her for his wife—her or no woman, present or to come. That rough wooings speed cheerily sometimes, witness King Harry the Fifth, or the son of "those fierce Vikings out of the dark Northeast," Hereward the Wake.

The staid atmosphere of St. Margaret's not having proved favorable to the growth of feminine coquetries, Lucy, trembling a little and blushing a great deal, but strong in trust, plighted him her troth.

Unlike the members of his adopted brotherhood in the New World, Tom Boynton never "calculated." He was quite unprepared for the effect of this news upon poor old Miss Boynton, who received his triumphant announcement with a sort of tearless grief peculiar to age, and most appealing to the stalwart mountaineer. He realized that to take Lucy away from her would be like tearing the ivy from a mouldering wall. To remain in England, as his aunt pleadingly suggested, partly dependent upon her slender means, until an opening in business could be found for him, was a thought impossible to entertain. Tom's heart went out with a mighty yearning towards the wonderful hill country left behind, and the prospect of speedy wealth it held out to a strong, capable fellow like himself.

For a time he was in a pitiful state of irresolution. One day in spring, when golden laburnums and sweet lilies-of-the-valley were coming out in the sunshine of the prim little garden behind the house, Tom strode up and down the walk, consumed with restlessness. Catching sight of Lucy's brown head at the window of the room where she sat sewing in a frame of ivy leaves, he asked her to put down her seam and come for a walk with him.

They reached a point beyond the town, where Lucy seated herself upon a bank of rich grass "with daisies pied," such as only England can produce. Looking down the vista of a bowery lane, they saw the minster tower rise ivy-wreathed against a tranquil sky, gray chimneys and moss-grown roofs clustering about it, half hidden from sight by venerable trees. A shining river ran through meadows of greenest turf. Everywhere the eye plunged into a mass of unequalled verdure. All was calm, hushed, locked in a deep repose. Here was old England garnering in her centuries of well-earned peace. Here, nearer still, was Lucy, her candid eyes fixed trustfully on his.

Just then the sun at setting painted the heavens with a glory unspeakable. It was as if his own Golden Gate had opened suddenly before him, and Tom sprang to his feet, the fire of "Westward Ho!" thrilling in his veins.

"Lucy," he cried, crushing her hands in his vigorous grasp—"dear, darling Lucy, it is an awful wrench, but I must go. It is only for a while, never fear; for while grass grows and water runs I'll be true to you, my lass. I am going to work for fortune now as I never did before. God bless your dear little soul, if there's gold to be had, I'll have it. Will you wait for me, Lucy?"

"I'll wait, Tom," she answered, simply.

"There is one thing you have never looked at,

my dear," said Tom, after a long talk over their plans. "It is just possible that you may be left alone in the world at a time when I can't get away to come for you. I am haunted by the fear. It drives me to proposing what I might not have dared to ask for otherwise. As my sweetheart, Lucy, you could not sail around the globe to come to me; but if you love me well enough to marry me now, before I go, and let me leave you the protection of my name, you can take ship at any time for New York, and from there take another to San Francisco, where I will meet my wife, and carry her off to my den in the mountains, like a great ogre as I am. Think twice, Lucy, before you say yes. It will be a long voyage for you, poor little waif, and a wild life after you get there: only—God forget me, Lucy, if I ever cease to love and cherish you as the apple of my eye!"

"I will do what you ask, Tom," Lucy said, like the creature of a dream.

Two years passed, and all that Lucy had to remind her of the strange vows she had taken were the little gold wedding ring he had squeezed upon her finger in the shadow of the old minster altar, another circlet hammered out of virgin Californian gold, and imprisoning a great sparkling diamond, sent after Tom's arrival in San Francisco, and the letters glowing with love and pride that came to her by every mail. Tom was now engineer in charge of a famous new mine up under the snow-peaks of the sierras, working hard and cheerily. Miss Boynton's little house overflowed with Indian, Mexican, and Chinese curiosities, quaint souvenirs of the far Pacific coast, and Lucy might have walked in silk attire had she chosen to assume the "marrowy shawls of China crape, like wrinkled skins on scalded milk," and their companion rolls of stuff, that Tom showered upon the two ladies from time to time.

Thus Lucy's even life ebbed on under the ivy-covered walls that bounded it.

When the day came that poor old Miss Boynton entered into everlasting rest, Lucy was bewildered by her sudden freedom, and the stirring change it entailed. She was an Englishwoman, however, which means one capable of arising to any emergency; and when the answer to the letter announcing her aunt's death to Tom arrived, it found her quite ready to obey its loving behest, and to set forth alone upon the two long voyages. Tom, who was chained to his post just then, awaited her with open arms.

Westward she journeyed bravely through Atlantic storms; then southward to the languid torpor of the tropic seas, and across the Isthmus to the calm Pacific. When at length the steamer passed through the Golden Gate into the broad land-locked harbor of San Francisco, Lucy's heart beat high with expectation. Enough of her story had become known to her fellow-voyagers to create in them a feeling of active sympathy in the expected reunion with her husband. Something very like a groan at his expense arose from Lucy's adherents when among all the motley groups of Californians, native and imported, assembled to greet the arrival of the ship, no trace appeared of the recreant Tom. Under the inspiration of Californian air, it is barely possible that Mrs. Boynton's zealous friends might at that point have been led to visit with prompt vengeance a laggard appearance of the missing man. If the quiver of Lucy's lip and her blanching cheek thus affected them, what would have been the result of witnessing the bitter, inconsolable burst of tears with which she shut herself in her state-room till the first disappointment was spent!

By the captain's advice, and under charge of respectable people, Lucy betook herself to a hotel, pending the arrival of tidings from her husband. It was evident that the letter announcing her coming, a date rendered previously uncertain by the settlement of her small business affairs in England, had miscarried. Her good friend the captain found for her a special opportunity to send a letter on to Tom without delay; and, Lucy's courage rising with renewed hope, she determined, after a day of rest, to take stage for the station nearest the mining camp, and there await his coming. The captain, who saw to all her arrangements and put her in the stage, watched her departure with glistening eyes. Lucy leaned out to wave her hand to him, "with a smile like an angel's," the old man afterwards declared.

During the first part of that long journey by stage Lucy knew not fatigue, so astonished and excited was she by the New-World glories. The early spring had broken up the gentle undulations of field and plain with countless flowering plants, whose fragrant breath perfumed the air. Far as the eye could reach in this wonderfully clarified atmosphere were vineyard-clad slopes, prosperous ranches, meadows dotted with patriarchal flocks and herds, and watered by crystal rivers. Above hung cliffs crowned with a dark continuous zone of pines, cutting off the flower-enamelled paradise below from the snow-shrouded crests of the sierras—"Tom's mountains," the foolish child called those grand untrodden summits. Lucy's insular reserve, her fears, her scruples, melted into the gladness of a child butterfly-hunting under a summer sun; her "heart clothed itself with love."

Something of her early exhilaration, but none of her patient courage, had worn away, when the unwonted fatigue of two days and a night of stage-riding took possession of Lucy's exhausted frame. A rough woman, her comrade during the greater part of the journey, had, to Lucy's unqualified despair, been left at the station before the terminus. She was alone now with half a dozen men, who surveyed her with curious but not irreverent eyes.

Jerry, the soft-voiced stage-driver, reined in his six magnificent horses with the same professional calm exhibited frequently during the journey in driving them at full gallop along the edge of a precipice.

The stage halted before the rude veranda of a desolate two-story building, with a little colony of out-houses to correspond, over which was proudly inscribed the word "Hotel." Lucy, almost unable to walk, was half carried across the threshold. The other passengers, travel-soiled as they were, rushed by her like so many cannon-balls into the open door-way of a supper-room, before which a stolid Chinaman promenaded back and forth ringing a resonant bell.

Making his obeisance to Lucy in the smoky, oil-reeking atmosphere of this sitting-room, bar, and office combined, stood the proprietor, a hopelessly seedy Don Quixote, with a smack of former gentility in his drawling tones.

"I am the wife of Mr. Boynton, of the Humboldt Mine," Lucy managed to say, with quiet dignity. "I have every reason to hope that my husband will meet me here very shortly, and I must beg you to give me a room at once where I may rest until he comes."

Although profuse in civilities upon the discovery that his guest was the "colonel's lady," as he chose, to Lucy's amusement, to style her, Don Quixote looked a trifle blank at the mention of a room. Going off for a moment into the supper-room, he quickly reappeared with the beaming announcement, made in the style of a provincial theatre manager, that "in order to accommodate Mrs. Colonel Boynton, Jedge Tompkins had kindly consented to double up with General Snyder for the night."

Lucy's strength only sufficed her to ascend to the rude room proffered by that distinguished citizen, Jedge Tompkins, and there to request a cup of tea. This awful beverage was served to her presently by the stolid Chinaman, who took the opportunity to remove a box of paper collars and a package of toothpicks belonging to the Judge, substituting for them Mrs. Boynton's rugs and dressing-case. Lucy waited to see him depart, bolted her door, spread one rug over the straw bed, and drew another upon herself as she dropped into the deep sleep of utter physical fatigue.

Towards morning she was aroused by a confused sound from the room below. She sprang up in bed, trying to realize her position. Through the thin boards dividing them she distinctly heard the rattle of dice-boxes, voices in dispute, oaths, a scuffle, a pistol shot, then another — a riot making hideous the night. Overcome with terror she tottered to her feet. The candle she had left burning flickered in its socket and went out, leaving her in darkness. Lucy groped her way to the window, with an absurd impulse to cry aloud for help. At the very moment when, fancying that she could detect the noise of a horse's hoofs, a wild prayer for Tom to come for her rose to her lips, more shots were heard below, and something whizzed up past her ear, leaving a trail like fire upon her cheek.

Tom Boynton, riding hard through the night over rough mountain-roads to seek his wife, reached the tavern just in time to find its inmates launched into a fierce but not unusual affray at cards. The landlord, apt at this stage of the game to be overcome by strong libations, and on the present occasion somewhat unnerved by what he called "the boys bein' rayther onexpectedly lively," directed him to Lucy's room. Tom's knock and call receiving no response, he burst open the door to find his wife lying senseless on the floor.

Out of her trance of terror Lucy slowly came. She felt the warm clasp of loving arms, a strong heart beating close to hers. A man's tears were rained upon her face, and the slight wound upon her cheek was stanched with tenderest kisses.

II

We may look in upon Lucy's new home, after the lapse of a peaceful year or two. It was a veritable mountain eyrie, somewhat apart from the mining settlement, a roughly built but comfortable cottage, clinging for dear life to the edge of a battlement of cliffs, nestled under the locked arms of giant pine-trees, where they lay down to rest at night lulled by the music of falling waters, in early spring swelling to the roar of a mighty cataract as the swollen torrent plunged downward through the cañon at their feet. As for the interior, every stick of furniture had been brought up on pack-mules from the station below, and it was not elaborate; but a few months of Lucy's stay sufficed to make of it a very bower of bliss, Tom thought. There were warm red curtains to hang before the casements, old Aunt Boynton's blue tea-cups and brass candlesticks for the dresser shelves, fair English linen and bright English silver adjusted by deftest English fingers upon their modest board. For drapery to the little lounge they had the brilliant coloring and fine web of blankets made by the Navajo Indians. How Lucy had cried for joy when she found blossoming bravely upon her window-sill a pot of old-fashioned red and white balsam, which Tom had raised for her from the seed, in memory of the garden at St. Margaret's!

As months went on, Lucy, well trained to the solitude of her New-World life, found a thousand charms surrounding it. In early summer, leaving their mossy fern-hung cliffs, Tom and she would make long expeditions on horseback down into the enchanting region, where, kneeling upon hillocks of emerald turf, waist-deep in scented grass, she might fill her lap with a mass of gaudy wild tulips, of lilies, and syringa lusciously sweet in smell, of tiny unknown flowers in every shade of blue and white and rose.

The glorious oaks of the foot-hill summits, spreading afar their layers of lustrous shade, appealed most strongly to her English heart; but she learned to look with enthusiasm upon the pines clothing with their girdle of everlasting green the granite ribs of the mountain monarchs couched in eternal sleep.

At last there came a late October day when Tom's baby-girl came into blossom like Alpine Edelweiss beneath a fall of snow. Lucy did well, and during two or three weeks purest love and joy reigned under the roof of the little dwelling. Tom walked about on tip-toes, and conversed in awe-stricken whispers even at the distance of a mile from his new treasure. An old Dutchwoman, who had been induced to come from a distant settlement to attend upon Lucy, abandoned them when the baby was about three weeks old, Lucy declaring herself quite strong enough to resume her usual duties about the cottage, aided by her quaint factotum, the Chinaman with a blue cotton blouse and a pigtail, who was their cook, launderer, and butler combined. A few days after, Tom bounded up the little path leading to his home, and burst in like an autumn blast of wind, to find Lucy sitting by the fire, looking pale and weary, holding her hand upon her side.

"I think I have taken a little cold, Tom," she said, trying to smile up at him in her usual fashion. "Perhaps I had better go back to bed."

And oh, the pity of it!—all too soon, poor little English Lucy lay still and cold upon her couch, the baby wailing at her side. Just before she died, Lucy asked Tom to listen—they were singing the "Jubilate" at St. Margaret's: so listening she passed away. They made her a grave at the foot of her favorite tree—a grand heaven-reaching pine, clothed with a mist of perfumed plumy green.

III

Tom Boynton recrossed his desolate threshold to cast himself down upon Lucy's vacant couch, and pray God to take him too. He heard a feeble cry, and felt beneath the clothes a stirring like the flutter of a bird. Lucy's baby lay there, forgotten in the might of his despair. He picked up the tiny thing, awkwardly adjusting its garments and soothing it against his cheek. The child cried on, and would not suffer him to lay it down; by-and-by it fell asleep in his bosom; and to his heart, that had been like a stone, there crept again a semblance of human warmth.

Next day storm-clouds hung low upon the peaks of the Sierras, and the wind went moaning through the pines. A miner, who was Tom's especial friend among his employés, came up early from the camp to find him making preparations for departure from the cottage.

Without proper food or attendance for the child, and with no prospect of securing for it a woman's care, short of the kind old nurse whose services at home were claimed by her own newly arrived grandchild, he had made up his mind, in view of the menacing snow blockade, to set out on horseback with the baby in his arms, and striking down the mountain-side by a precipitous trail not often used, make all speed to gain the far-away ranch-house where the old nurse might be found. Tom's mare, the noble creature that had borne him so fleetly and so faithfully to meet his bride, was equipped with such provision for the ride as she could carry, and the infant, warmly wrapped, was laid in her father's breast. Boynton rode forth from his home into the forest gloom, like a spirit driven from paradise, daring not to look behind.

With steady riding, under ordinary conditions of the weather, he might hope by evening to secure a shelter for the child. A sullen canopy of sky and a peculiar threatening of snow in the atmosphere caused him many an anxious pang of doubt and self-reproach as from time to time he gazed in upon the sleeping baby nestled under the folds of the great plaid with which she was bound to his body, then, loosening rein, let the mare out into a long even stride, carrying them swiftly through the pine-carpeted forest reaches, and across the granite ledges, where her hoofs rang cheerily.

A snow-flake, then another, fell like lead upon his heart. They came thick and fast as the short day closed in, bringing the expedition to a sudden halt. The dreaded snow was upon them in good earnest, and he dared not risk the loss of trail. Turning aside under the impervious roofing of a group of firs, Boynton prepared to bivouac.

No hardship this for an old campaigner, and in a short time a brisk flame from a pile of storm-riven logs and branches shot up into the blue shadows overhead. Tom would have taken oath that his brave little comrade smiled back at him when, after feeding, he stowed her warmly away, under the peak of an India rubber blanket, upon a royally fragrant couch of moss and fir boughs. She lay there, uttering a few inarticulate murmurs of sweet content, while he brewed himself a pot of tea, and looked after the comfort of his mare, tethered sociably at his elbow.

Through the long watches of the night, while Tom kept vigil by his baby's side, taking anxious heed of the progress of the storm, his faithful animal turned on him eyes so full of human sympathy he almost felt that she must speak.

With the return of daylight Boynton determined at all cost to take up the abandoned trail. Cheering him as could no other sound, arose the baby's lusty demand for breakfast. Making nervous haste to prepare for her a meal consisting of biscuit-crumbs and sugar, with snow-water warmed over the embers, he broke camp, and set forth anew upon his eyrie pilgrimage.

Amid the spectral tree-forms shivering beneath their weight of snow (his knowledge of the conformation of the hills, the grouping of the rocks, aiding him in this extremity) he labored on, progress at every moment becoming more difficult, in the teeth of a growing storm. The mare's feet gathered snow until, sliding forward with a dangerous rush down the incline, then pulling herself up, with panting sides, she would turn her head away from the furious onslaught of wind and snow bearing upon them through the forest aisles like a wall of breakers on the shore.

Tom Boynton drew rein beneath an overhanging shelf of rock, not knowing whether he had there found his grave and his child's. Hour after hour, while the sleet drove and the wind raged, he stood with his back against the granite wall, hugging the baby close, wetting her lips with wine, and breathing his warm breath on her face. With all his might he resisted an overmastering sense of drowsiness. The recklessness of life before possessing him was merged into an intense desire to struggle for existence for the sake of Lucy's little one, Once, when the baby cried long and piteously, Tom sang her to rest with the fragment of a nursery song, the big tears running down his cheeks.

The storm lulled, and the sleet-fall changed into rain as the afternoon wore on. Bad as the outlook was, the situation left him no alternative but to press forward with all the strength remaining to man and beast. Down in the valley below this ridge was a familiar ford, beyond which he knew the locality to have been a recent camping ground for Indians. Again they set out under clouds closing down in a dense gray curtain, to break ere long into a violent pelting shower of rain. In a moment Boynton was soaking wet, as if he had fallen in a stream. The baby, roused to a new sense of discomfort, uttered a faint moan. Looking in upon her, he saw a strange pallor on the little face, a blue shade settling on her lips.

Now, indeed, Tom Boynton's stout heart quailed within him. They had reached the summit of the mountain spur. Below, chafing within its rocky bed, ran the turbulent river. Over upon the farther bank, curling merrily up among a thicket of firs, arose the unmistakable column of a camp-fire smoke.

With a shout to his mare, Tom dashed madly down the hill. For Lucy's dear sake he would gain that camp with her child alive!

With her fine instinct of never-flagging sympathy, the mare plunged unhesitatingly into the icy stream. Then ensued a rare struggle, every nerve of horse and rider strained to keep afloat under the fierce resistance of the swollen torrent. About mid-stream the mare was caught in the waves and whirled about like a cork. Boynton threw himself into the boiling foam, and, supporting his precious freight upon the saddle with one hand, managed to keep up with the other, until, by a splendid effort, the mare recovered her balance and struck out for the shore, planting her hoofs in triumph upon firm ground at last.

Tom rode into the Indian encampment, where a half-dozen of them were busy around a generous fire of logs. A young woman, tall, impassive, stately, like a Diana cast in bronze, looked up from her pappoose at the apparition of this spent and dripping traveller, who could only muster strength to drop from his saddle, walk into the red glare of the heavenly ring of warmth, and without words hold out to her the burden from his breast.

IV

A FEW years ago some Americans newly arrived in Paris were lounging in the court-yard of the Grand Hôtel, listening to the idle talk of their compatriots, who dispensed with liberal hand the gossip of their colony.

While they were thus chatting a carriage drove under the *porte-cochère*, from which an elaborate footman proceeded to extract severally a middle-aged gentleman of distinguished appearance, a lady bountifully handsome, cordial in manner, frankly magnificent in attire, and a young girl dressed in gray velvet with bands of silvery gray fur, the type of whose aristocratic beauty would have stamped her as worthy of adorning any court in Europe.

As this party passed in all of the young men doffed their hats. One of them stood as if moonstruck by the vision.

"Hamersly, you are palpably slain on the spot; or is it the reopening of some old wound? You have met our American 'Edelweiss,' the 'rare pale Margaret,' before?"

"I did not know I am a fanatic," said Hamersly, coming out of his maze; "I honestly declare to you that I never in all my life till now saw a girl before whom I felt madly inclined to throw myself down and be trampled on."

"You may be saved the sacrifice, my dear fellow," his friend said, with the pleased air of one who has a sensation to communicate. "Can it be that the joy is reserved for me of finding one man in Paris who doesn't know that the young lady you have just seen is in a few days to become by her marriage with the Duc de B—— a member of one of the most illustrious families in France?—that he is as romantically in love with her as if he were the poorest and proudest of *jeunes premiers*, which, indeed, he might be from his looks?—that the handsome old fellow yonder, with the sort of cavalier dash about him, and those ferocious long mustaches and melancholy eyes, is her father, who worships the ground she treads upon—a father-in-law many a man besides the Duc has coveted, let me tell you—Tom Boynton, the Californian millionaire, the well-beloved hero of the Pacific coast?"

"And the florid lady is her mother, I suppose?"

"Nothing of the sort. You are arguing yourself unknown not to recognize the famous Queen of Diamonds of our colony, who has a very substantial husband of her own hereabouts. Miss Boynton has had the benefit of her chaperonage off and on since leaving her *pensionnat* a year ago. Old Tom Boynton married, indeed. Half the women of your acquaintance would tell you how unlikely that is ever to come to pass again."

GOLDEN-ROD

GOLDEN-ROD:

An Idyl of Mount Desert

I

It was at one of the "Patriarchs'" balls at Delmonico's, two seasons ago, that Erskine first saw the woman destined to reign upon the empty throne of his affections.

He had been poor, proud, and studious during many years of his college life and subsequent career at the New York bar, had abjured society as far too expensive a luxury, and, with the exception of dining occasionally with two or three warm friends, who would not take "no" for an answer, went nowhere.

The windfall of an unexpected inheritance, leading to a summer run over the European Continent, where he fell into the hands of Mrs. Pratt (Polly Pratt, she is commonly called by her followers), extracted him from his seclusion as cleanly as a nut kernel from its shell. Mrs. Pratt has a way with her that no one can resist, and the two or three fashionable New York girls in her train fell upon this "new" man with the rapture that inspired Columbus when he first saw the coast-line of the New World detached from the waste of waters. Erskine was whizzed through Switzerland and Germany with lightning speed, and taken to see the midnight sun in company with all these gay, gossiping people, who flattered him so delicately that, only in the most imperceptible way, he awoke one morning to find himself a desirable, fresh from the mint, and ready to be put into immediate circulation in the society of the great Western metropolis.

When they all met again, in December, in New York, Erskine was more and more filled with surprise that he had not long ago found out how very nice it is to dine, day after day, with charming well-bred people, in houses that are a dream of decorative art; to drop in at one or two clubs, and chat with fellows who are ever ready to "put you up to anything;" to ride up the Avenue and through the Park, past long lines of elegant equipages, whence gay nods and wooing smiles are bestowed in quick succession.

To weary women and responsive girls this man was a heaven-send, with his erect figure, his warm coloring, his clear eye, his look of active manhood, and strong intelligence. Then, too, while conscious of his success, he had the rare grace to be modest in his hour of triumph. As yet the insufferable airs of some young Knickerbockers had not invaded him. Perhaps it was a relic of his barbarism that made him laugh naturally, walk with a spring in his step, treat women with an old-fashioned chivalrous courtesy, and deal with a young girl in thought and speech as with a sister.

Not one of all the women of the world whom he had met had as yet had power to quicken his pulses, until one evening, at the February ball I speak of, he saw Rosalie Gray leave her seat upon the dais, where she was talking to an effusive old dowager, and, laying her hand upon some man's coat-sleeve with the coldest touch imaginable, go out to join the dance. She had refused to dance in the cotillon, and it was apparently to supplant one reign of boredom by another that she made this move.

Erskine stood gazing at her tall form, draped in white, with a glitter like that of the snow in moonlight, her bust rising and falling tranquilly under a circlet of diamonds, her proud head undecked, save by a few jewelled stars. He was quite too recent a recruit to the privileged ranks of the Patriarchs to know that she was the best-dressed woman in the room. It was left to little Watson Webster at his elbow to appraise her gown, to affix the great maker's name, to reckon up the value of her gems, to speculate as to who had sent her the two bouquets she carried—one of royal red Jacqueminot roses, the other of

> "naiad-like lilies of the vale,
> Whom youth makes so fair and passion so pale
> That the light of their tremulous bells is seen
> Through their pavilions of tender green."

Erskine saw her lend herself haughtily to the arm of her *danseur*, and melt away into the throng, with an insane jealousy of the puppy who dared invade this goddess by a touch. Eagerly did his eyes follow her perfect grace, and all the while Watson Webster continued to babble in his ear unweariedly.

Watson is the most industrious of quidnuncs, and a more useful small personage to society it would be difficult to find. He is kind and gracious to all the débutantes, and hand in glove with all the dowagers. He fancies that half of them are secretly in love with him, but, like Mr. Snevellicci, he is catholic in his admirations, and says, "I love 'em, every one." While Watson stands, with his little cock-sparrow air and his eye-glasses, talking of fifty things, poor moon-struck Erskine, losing sight of his beauty as she passes out under the soft pink-shaded lamps into another room, turns upon him with a gasp.

"Who is she?" he asks, as if there was but one "divinest she" in all this throng.

"Oh, really, now, my dear fellow!" remonstrates Mr. Webster, with a puzzled air; and when Erskine makes him understand, he speaks relentingly. "Oh, that, indeed! Well, I'm not surprised, as you are just beginning among us, and she keeps to herself awfully. That's Mrs. Gaspar Gray, a widow, who has been in Europe, mending her broken heart, as we Americans always do, for several years. People are making no end of fuss over her this season, but somehow or other I don't seem to get on with her. That grand sort of creature is all very well, you know, but to my taste a woman should be 'simpatica;' that's it—'simpatica,' you know."

Watson was quite delighted with himself for finding so elegant a phrase, and went on cheerfully:

"She made an immense success in London last spring, and at Newport this summer, when she came back. She has a beautiful house in —— Street, but don't take the trouble to entertain much. Now dinners, for instance—a widow ought, in my opinion, to lay herself out on dinners. It is her mission in life, according to my idea. As far as you are concerned, I don't see how you are to get the entrée there, because, for one thing, you are handicapped by that Pratt set. Mrs. Gaspar Gray sits on that kind of thing awfully. I advise you to be very careful, my dear fellow, about that kind of thing. You can't be too particular to know *just* the right sort of people at the start, and stick to them."

Little Watson was so plaintive in his admonitions that Erskine laughed outright. To him the spectacle of these society men, so decorous, so languid, so anxious to step neither to the right nor to the left of the chalk line described for the division of their "set" from the next—so terribly in earnest about it all—was infinitely diverting.

When he made his way into the supper-room, it was to be hailed by Mrs. Pratt, who, in a gown all pink and blue, with roses, like a Dresden figurine, had taken possession of a table in company with two or three fast girls and men. This little lady is in her element when reigning over a supper-table at a ball. She has a talent for venturing to the verge and not falling over that is quite unparalleled; and being well-born, rich, and supplied with a most complaisant husband, is in the front rank of good society. With Erskine she had always been endlessly good-natured, sisterly, and on her guard. To-night he felt as if he hardly knew her for the same woman. She drew aside her gauzy clouds of blue and rose-color, calling him to sit by her; she had a bottle of champagne in her hand, and filled from it a goblet, which she held to Erskine's lips, and a fire of raillery arose from all the gay party, which, so far from exhilarating him, excited the profoundest gloom.

At the very moment when he was thus coldly captive, Mrs. Gaspar Gray, with a distinguished-looking gray-haired gentleman for her cavalier, than whom there is no one more honored in the community, whose word is law in all matters of social observance, passed them by. Her dress brushed Erskine, and a floating fringe caught and was fixed upon the button of his coat. He sprang to his feet and endeavored to aid her in withdrawing it; Mrs. Pratt, also, transformed into a busy ingenuous fairy, proffering her services. It was curious to note the look upon Rosalie Gray's face as she calmly repelled the advances of Mrs. Pratt's coterie. Had they been disembodied spirits she could not have looked *through* them more completely. But when the link binding her to Erskine refused to break, and some one was searching for a penknife to cut the Gordian knot, the horror of a scene, and in such company, overcame Mrs. Gray so far as to bring a flush to her features like the rosy sunrise on Mont Blanc. Erskine could hardly tell whether she even noticed him, as she stood there erect, with her proudly-poised head and delicately-curved nostrils, impatient to be gone. For one moment their eyes met, as he bowed low, and she swept away.

For the rest of the evening Erskine was on thorns. He watched her surrounded by men, and with resentment observed that she danced twice again—once with the Vicomte de Marsac, a Frenchman of distinction on his American travels; once with Mr. Vernon, a statuesque creature contributed to the evening's entertainment by her Majesty's legation at Washington, which was supposed to claim the right to his valuable services at other times.

In vain did Mrs. Pratt resume her winning courtesies. Erskine felt unconquerably oppressed by her and by everything. He haunted the corridor, and, when a tall figure draped in a white and gold wrap went down the stairs, again attended by the gentleman who took her to the supper-room, Erskine, with ulster on and hat in hand, found his way to the lower landing. Fate favored him, for just as Mr. A——, whom he knew, reached the last step, he slipped and twisted his foot, making it necessary to be at least assisted to a seat. Erskine's offer of service to him was courteously declined, but as the door opened and "Mrs. Gaspar Gray's carriage" was loudly announced, her footman appearing outside, Mr. A—— said, hurriedly,

"Put Mrs. Gray in the carriage for me, Erskine, will you? I shall be all right in ten minutes, I assure you, Mrs. Gray. A thousand thanks for your solicitude. Oh, I beg your pardon! May I introduce to you my friend, Mr. Erskine—Mrs. Gaspar Gray?"

It was done: for a moment her gloved fingers touched his hand. She entered her carriage, the footman closed the door; there was a cool conventional murmur of "thanks" bestowed upon poor Erskine, with hardly a glance towards him, as the little brougham, crowded in the line, drove off rapidly, leaving him with a vision of a clear-cut face looking out of the white and gold draperies, and a waft of odor from the roses and lilies in her hand that will haunt him all his life.

And then, as it often happens we meet people once whom we have never seen before, and go on meeting them pertinaciously, Erskine encountered Rosalie Gray within two days after that. He was behind time at a large dinner-party, and reached the drawing-room only to be assigned to a pretty young girl of the period, so confident of her own powers, and so full of easy talk, that during two hours he abandoned the thought of any possible exertion other than that necessary to the consideration of Mrs. Lyle's perfect menu.

"This has been such a gay season, you can't think," Miss Amy North was saying in his ear, while addicting herself with the frank gourmandize of girlhood to a *bouchée à la reine*, "this is my tenth large dinner, and I have been to fourteen lunches already. I can't count the dances and little things, and as to afternoon teas, they are a nuisance; don't you think so? I never saw you at an afternoon tea, by-the-way. I think they are just a sort of an apology for people who don't know how to entertain, getting Robinson to send cards to everybody they know, giving them bread-and-milk all around, and then patting them on the head, and telling them to run home early and go to bed, like good children."

"A sort of a curfew bell for society?" Erskine said, laughing at her strictures. "I don't see how you accomplish anything else but winging your way from one flower to another in such a life as this."

"Oh, I haven't told you half," said Miss Amy, with disdain. "Why, all the girls in my set do a great deal more than that. We have a Shakespeare class and a German class and a literature class. Then we go to draw at the Art League, and to do crewel-work at the Decorative Art Society. Then we must go to that dear Theodore Thomas's concerts, you know, and I have my singing twice a week with Herr Bayreuth. What with the theatre now and then—it's so nice to go to Wallack's, and there is always something melodramatic for you to cry over (if you can, but I *can't*) at the Union Square — and lots of other things, one's time is pretty well taken up."

"How much I should value that portion of it you are bestowing now upon me!"

"Oh, I like to talk to you," was the consoling rejoinder. "The truth is, my brother-in-law, Frank Thornton, and Gracie (that's his wife, my sister, you know) had made such a swan of you before I ever met you that I was rather inclined to think you horrid. You know how one feels about those people in Sunday-school books who *love* to take their medicine, and *want* to die early, and all that sort of thing? I had a kind of an idea that you would be like that; but it is quite different. Gracie says when you come to see us she always feels as if somebody had opened a door in a very hot room. *Filet*? No, thanks, and no champagne. It is my principle always to skip here till we come to the salad at a dinner. That and an ice-pudding are like oases in the desert of Sahara. Do you know I am seriously thinking of retiring from the world after this year? One likes to try everything, of course, but one or two seasons will be enough for me. I can stand the girls, and some of the men; but I have no patience with the older women—the married ones; they take everything away from us in New York society."

"There is a remedy that I observe most of you young ladies fly to," Erskine said, with a smile.

"Well, but if I loved anybody, as Grace loves Frank, for example," said Amy, with a look like Una's in her face, "I should want to stay with him and read, and go to balls together and come away early, as they do. But these women who are rather old—at least I think so—who go around to public places with silly little boys—keeping Kindergarten, we girls call it. Look at Mrs. Pratt. Almost any man is game for her, and you see her with everybody in turn. There is one woman in town whom I admire more than anybody else, and there she is, at the very end of the table, next to Mr. Lyle. You can't see her for those waxlights. Lean this way a moment. Isn't she a love?—Mrs. Gaspar Gray."

Far up the glittering vista of lights and glass and porcelain, over a bed of Maréchal Neil roses, Erskine saw her beautiful, high-bred face, wearing a little wearied air that charmed and excited him at once. His heart beat high with the anticipation of meeting her again.

"Why, what is the matter?" said the quick-sighted Miss Amy. "You look wonderfully bright. One would think that you belong to Mrs. Gray's cordon of unrequited lovers."

"I have never spoken to her in my life," he said, gayly. "May I not worship from afar? The ladies are going, I see. *Au revoir*, then, in the drawing-room."

The long train of beautiful women passed out. When the men rejoined them, the large room, sparkling with the subdued light of many candles, set upon mantel-shelf and brackets everywhere, and in sconces of old English brass high up on walls hung in the half-tints of color that artists love, displayed more than one group of beauties a man might cheerfully delay to look upon. Erskine had eyes but for one. Against a portière of Oriental stuff of some deep blue, like the plum before a touch has brushed away its silvery bloom, sat Rosalie Gray. Her dress was of a pale yellow brocade, the front of palest blue. Round her throat was a necklet of diamonds, and at her breast a great cluster of early jonquils nestled in the folds of some rare old Venice point. Her hand trifled with a pale blue fan, with carved sticks of yellow ivory. She was in conversation with Mrs. Lyle, but arose as the gentlemen came in, and, making her adieus, quickly disappeared.

"Another engagement," the hostess said, when some one asked the reason why.

"That is the penalty of wooing a bright particular star," was the laughing rejoinder. "Nobody is so much in demand as Mrs. Gray."

Bitterly disappointed, Erskine sought the street. It was drizzling gently as he walked down the avenue to his club, but he did not know it until, upon going into the smoking-room, some acquaintance suggested to him that he had better go home to change his clothes.

Something possessed him next day to go to a famous florist and wreck himself upon an order for roses—rare, princely roses, laid layer upon layer in beds of maidenhair fern. These were sent anonymously to her address, and for weeks the offering was repeated, until the florist and his young man began to look upon this reckless youth with the favor bestowed only upon male customers either just before or for a short time after their entrance into the holy estate of matrimony.

He saw her in her brougham in the Park; on horseback sometimes, followed by her groom; at the opera, where from a distant door-way he gazed at her profile against the crimson lining of her box, fancied that he saw his flowers in her hand, and noted with exultation that among all the visitors succeeding each other in the vacant chairs behind her there was not one to whom she gave a shade of preference above the rest.

At last, one morning when he was coming out of the Brunswick, a lady walking with a firm, light tread crossed his path. She looked up, and for the first time since their casual introduction met his open gaze. Alas for Erskine and all his wasted hopes and roses! Mrs. Gaspar Gray looked at him without a shadow of recognition in her glorious eyes. He might have been the jaunty porter of the Hotel Brunswick, standing near, for all interest she vouchsafed.

"It is over," Erskine said, between his teeth, striding away over Madison Square.

II

ONE summer evening, when town had become rather less endurable than usual with heat and dust, Erskine dropped in upon a pair of people of his acquaintance, to whom you were very irregularly presented by Miss Amy North, in the last chapter, as " Frank and Gracie."

Erskine found them fanning themselves in the half-light of a parlor open on all sides to what stirring of the air it was possible to trap under the semblance of a breeze. An exhausted voice came to him in greeting from a gilt wicker-chair, and he felt his way to a small jewel-laden hand, though not without becoming entangled in a billowy mass of lawn and lace that lay across the India-matting.

"I am as glad to see you as I can be of anything in this weather," Mrs. Thornton said. " Pray sit here between the windows, and have a fan. Frank dear, are you *quite* sure that you have opened everything, and will you please take away these flowers from my side ?"

"'I hate these roses' feverish blood,'" quoted obedient Frank, as he bore away the vase whose fragrance was filling all the air. " Erskine, we have just arrived at that period of matrimonial debate when we welcome an outsider. My wife is becoming a little plaintive, and I a little argumentative. Amy, who has no fancy for this atmosphere of domestic gloom, has retired up-stairs, I believe, to read some book upon arctic explorations, which she finds a solace on a day like this. The point at issue is, What shall we do to get out of town, and where shall we go? Here am I, with a nursery full of whooping-cough and incipient teeth, which very naturally militate against a warm reception for us anywhere; a charming sister-in-law, who must have the usual diversion of woman in her hours of ease; an adorably patient wife, who has submitted to the untold sacrifice of staying in town until nearly the end of June."

"We are growing positively cross under the protracted indecision," Mrs. Thornton said. "We talk of a dozen plans, and never can agree on one for five minutes at a time. I am afraid"—this was ventured soothingly—"Frank *rather* dreads a long journey anywhere just now."

"Rather," said Frank, grimly. "Juvenile demands for paternal ministrations, however sweet in the sacred seclusion of one's own nursery, do not, as a rule, excite either pride or joy in the bosom of a man who must promenade forever back and forth through a railway car, with sandwiches and silver cups of water, during all the thousand hours of a slowly waning midsummer day. But here comes Amy to lend her voice. Can you discover Mr. Erskine, Amy, in this uncertain light?"

Erskine advanced to meet the slight, erect figure, to be welcomed in her somewhat high-pitched but clear and pleasant voice.

"I am not quite sure, Frank dear, that I mean to be altogether civil to Mr. Erskine, after the evening last winter when I talked *at* him, from the oysters to the coffee, at Mrs. Lyle's dinner, and he basely took himself off without even bidding me good-night."

Erskine remembered this occasion well enough to feel a sharp pang at having it recalled. He threw himself upon the young lady's mercy, and was sufficiently forgiven to have her take a seat near him by the window, where the light from a street lamp streamed across her cool pink muslin gown, her bare round arms, with elbow sleeves, and her prim little white lace fichu with the pink rose and knots of black velvet.

"All will be forgiven and forgotten," said Miss Amy, "if you will only help me to coax or coerce this wretched Frank and Gracie into submission to my will. Give ear unto me, O ye people, while I test my eloquence! Imagine, then, being perched on the deck of a yacht that skims like a sea-gull over lovely little crested waves along the coast of Maine. Every now and then a dash of salt spray flies up on your feet and petticoats—"

"I can't imagine it, Amy," said Frank.

"(Don't, Frank, for I am going to be really impressive)—but you don't mind it a bit, for there is the most agreeable man conceivable—generally from Boston—"

"Thanks," said both of the gentlemen from New York.

"—at your feet, quoting Tennyson's 'Voyage,' as he gazes up at you. The yacht speeds gloriously on her way before a stiff breeze through a region of sea and mountain, crag and pebbly beach. All the crimps come out of your hair; anchovy sandwiches and claret-cup are passed about; everything is delightful—when suddenly the jib-boom, or whatever the nasty thing is, comes sweeping round, and everybody has to get up and change places, and ten to one another girl gets your man."

"You are becoming too personal, Amy, to accomplish your point," her sister said, while they all laughed at her nonsense.

"Well, if that don't tempt you, think of canoeing over to Bar Island on a midsummer day. Of standing on the top of Green Mountain in a breeze. Of sitting under the cliffs at The Ovens, and watching the boats go by. Of catching trout in Eagle Lake. Of riding in a buck-board and shouting 'Nancy Lee.' Tell me, if you dare, individually or collectively, that there is anything better for us to do than to go to Mount Desert?"

"You have omitted one of the hotel joys," said her brother (The Counsellor, as he was called by most of his friends)—"that of being served with mackerel and doughnuts at the hands of a disguised princess wearing a celluloid coronet. I remember once asking my particular one of these stately attendants what her name was. 'My name is Mrs. Somerset,' she remarked, with withering dignity. 'But them as knows me well calls me Sairey.'"

The talk, turned into this channel, went on until town—its gaslights, the sidewalks where hot haggard-looking people went wandering by, and wan little tenement-house children crept out to play until far into the night, the roll of vehicles and tinkling street-car bells—had melted away like the scene of a theatre, to be replaced by country visions cool and beautiful, where

"Only to hear and see the far-off sparkling brine—
Only to hear were sweet, stretched out beneath the pine."

"You have conquered, Amy," suddenly remarked The Counsellor. "It is evident that we have all talked ourselves into a state of mind for which there is no cure save our beloved Bar Harbor. I have been turning over in my brain a plan I have had proposed to me to abridge the distance, or to modify the weariness of the jaunt to those slumbering cherubs up-stairs. I think I have hit it exactly. And to put it out of the power of any one to misinterpret me, or to tell me afterwards that I never can make myself clearly understood—"

"That I never did," said his wife, with fervor.

"—I hereby pledge myself to conduct you all, after a method of my own, as far as Boston. Only I stipulate that no questions be asked; that we start this day week; that we don't go a step unless

Erskine be of the party; that I am for once captain of my crew, with undisputed powers. You consent, Grace, Amy, and Erskine? Then let us ring for Apollinaris water, and hurrah for the Thornton family *en voyage!*"

III

THE day before the eve of our great national holiday, when all New York lay simmering with heat and patriotic zeal, ready to boil over on the glorious Fourth, saw the Thornton family upon the steps of their home in one of the avenues, delivering the keys of the house into custody of the melancholy female in a crushed bonnet, whose sad lot it was to remain during the next three months entombed in an atmosphere of brown holland, tête-à-tête with household gods swathed in white or shrouded with mosquito gauze.

The children, from the front seat of the carriage, behind a breastwork of rugs, bags, and umbrellas, vociferously condoled with that dejected personage, who stood courtesying within the vestibule. Their elders—Mr. Thornton in a cab, intending to pick up Erskine at his club, who got in with a parting look at the mountain of luggage completely obscuring from view both horses and driver of an express wagon—were themselves pervaded with a sense of benevolent pity for all stay-at-homes of whatever estate in life.

As they drove down Broadway after a halt for fruit and cigars, the great business world was palpitating through its daily task at the mercy of a withering sun. From Grace Church to Rector Street, where the carriage turned from the whirl of Broadway into a region tinctured with the old-time dignity lingering upon the flanks of Trinity Church, they met a continuous line of vehicles so apparently tangled in wild confusion that the chief dangers of the route seemed to attend our travellers at the outset.

Beside the pier where they finally drew up a large coasting steamer, just about to sail, awaited them.

"Here we are," said The Counsellor, radiantly. "All aboard, if you please, ladies and gentlemen. Until we reach Boston, at least, there will be room enough in the world for my restless young family."

The gloomy wharf over which their procession passed presented an appearance very unlike those most known to New York voyagers, where several times a week gay birds of passage flutter, to be wafted on their ocean voyages with flowers and waving handkerchiefs; it was encumbered with huge trucks loading or unloading freight.

The large dimensions of the steamer afforded no small consolation to the depressed matron of the party, when she presently found herself politely assisted up what seemed Jacob's own ladder hanging in mid-air, and when her Blessed Baby had been safely hoisted after her. Across a broad clean after-deck, through the cabin, where tea was in readiness, they were conducted to spacious and airy state-rooms. Nothing was lacking for comfort. These favored mortals were guests of the line—the only passengers—and, through the courtesy of the owners, monarchs of all they surveyed for the next twenty-eight or thirty hours.

As they unpacked and disposed of their traps the ship parted company with her berth, and noiselessly glided out into the river. The absence of all the customary bustle at such a moment was curious enough. Hardly a sound broke the silence from either the steamer or the wharf. It was like embarking in a phantom ship, and "quite deliciously mysterious," as Amy North observed.

Rounding the Battery, New York, with all her sins and excited thermometers, lay behind them; her towers and spires piercing through golden mist, her shipping alive with the commerce of the world. Under the wonderful arch of the Brooklyn Bridge they slid like a snake, and thence fresh winds, sighed for in vain during the sultry days just gone, wafted them on their way. Into the troubled waters of Hell Gate, now lulled to repose by a spell more enduring than that which controlled the raging Kuhleborn, leaving behind those beautiful islands condemned to the mournful uses of mad-houses, hospitals, reformatories and prison cells; along the emerald shores of Astoria, and so close to the fringe of salt-meadow encircling the old Morrisania mansion that they seemed to be heading straight into the rose-wreathed pillars of its ancient veranda; past Port Morris, and over the spot where the British troop-ship went down, with her store of gold sent out to pay the redcoats in the Revolutionary War. And thus gliding on, over water so still and shining that sea and sky seemed blended into one, and inhaling soft land-breezes, fraught with sweet odors of new-mown hay, that touched the brow with a thrilling caress, they heard the sunset gun boom from Fort Schuyler, and watched the evening-star trembling into light.

The little ones, who had romped over the deck, sniffing the pure sea-breeze, until already a redder tinge had come into their cheeks, retired to rest with cheerful unconcern of their surroundings. A double berth received the younger two, dexterously imbedded at either end, like apples in a dumpling. No apparition of the terrors of Point Judith assailed them, as through the long bright summer night the steamer ploughed peacefully over the smooth waters of the Sound. Not so fared Mrs. Thornton, who, having announced that she should be sick while skirting that "still-vex'd Bermoothes," had made up her mind to fulfil the prophecy at any cost, and was naturally indignant when not the least excuse offered for doing so. Amy declared of Grace that she was like the old lady of blessed memory who always slept with an umbrella and galoshes, to be ready for every emergency. So she braced herself for the tribulation that ought to have come, and about four o'clock in the morning arose resolutely, made her toilet with unshrinking hand, and went out on deck to battle with the foe. Boisterous Point Judith was asleep and peaceable enough, but the witchery of the scene, reluctantly abandoned late the night before, was gone. The deck was saturated by fog, shutting out all about them, save the long billows softly powdered with yeasty foam from the ship's sides. Everything was woe-begone. An occasional sailor gave the only evidence of life, and he slunk by her, dripping. Moisture exuded from every pore of the ship; the rigging streamed with it, and comfort was nowhere to be found. In the desolation of the moment a qualm of sea-sickness would have been almost a relief. But no; nothing suggested itself but a feeling of general forlornness, induced by the hour and the outlook. It was not until the benevolent steward, observing this solitary waif on deck, had brought a cup of tea and a ship-biscuit that Mrs. Thornton's spirits rose to a level the plummet could fathom. She needed them all to meet the merciless banter that awaited her from her husband.

When breakfast was ready the rest of the party appeared, looking generally bright and hearty. They sat around the captain's table, on high stools, like school-boys *en pénitence;* and then it was that Blessed Baby revelled in unwonted dishes, bolting, Amy asserted, a "plumbiferous doughnut" and a pickled cucumber, as the polite steward, according him a dignity hitherto unattained, deferentially handed everything in turn.

The officers of the ship, clustered around the lower end of the table, formed a characteristic group. Distinctively American in feature, they sat in serious, almost melancholy, silence, eagerly discussing a variety of dishes. The captain—a gruff, hearty man, bearded like a pard—was scarcely seen in the cabin during the voyage, but addicted himself to the pilot-house, with a watchful devotion to duty as a navigator, which explained the fact that, amid the many dangers of fogs and shoals, there had been for eight years not one accident to a ship of this line. "Never see the captain down below when there's a fog like this," remarked one of the officers—an announcement as cheering as anything could be in a "fog like this."

Dreary enough is this phase of coast-voyaging, and against it one may never be altogether secure.

When Point Judith was left behind, and the ship had sailed into Vineyard Sound, the gray curtain hung heavy around them, and the hoarse, discordant whistle kept calling, to be answered by whistle or bell from shore or light-ship, or by the whistle of a steamer or the horn of a sailing vessel, near by but invisible. The sun struggled sharply with the fog, and from time to time conquered it, the envious drapery lifting for an instant to reveal picturesque glimpses of the main-land, or of the camp-meeting grounds at Martha's Vineyard, where the white roofs rising amid foliage, and the green waters of a little bay dancing in the sunlight, fairly dazzled the eyes with brightness. At such a moment the fog melted away as if by magic; the constant vigil of the lookout in the bows was relaxed; the raucous whistle of the steam-pipe ceased; the decks were dried by sparkling sunshine; a fresh breeze enlivened everything; the order was given to go ahead, and the ship fairly sprung forward in a merry race with the crested billows. Our party, gathered under an awning on deck, felt the general exultation. The Counsellor rebounded from the pressure of feminine reproaches heaped upon him during the fog, because, forsooth, he had decoyed his family into *cette galère*. He took heart of grace now, and waxed facetious, aiming witticisms at his tormentor, who somewhat reluctantly consented to smile once more. Amy and Erskine walked vigorously up and down the decks. The children, happy beings, had rioted madly all day—into the rigging, on top of the awning, everywhere—had romped with their father, their aunty, and Erskine, and had made frequent visits to the steward and the two black cooks, which generally resulted in pockets stuffed with edibles. Even the Blessed Baby, emulating his predecessors, toddled off on excursions of his own devising, and parleyed with the smiling darkies, who leaned out of the galley windows, affecting an inability to interpret the assiduous repetition of "Cookey, cakey," pronounced in every accent from entreaty to command. Their maid had quite as much exercise in that one day as was good for her, following the vagaries and suppressing the dangerous freaks of her youthful charges.

The only officer to be seen on the after-deck was the chief engineer, who, like a whale coming to the surface for an occasional breath of air, ascended now and then from cavernous depths, where, as the children were told by Erskine, he had charge of a mighty monster which, attended by half a dozen slaves to feed it on live coals, lay chained at the bottom of the ship. A zealous politician was the chief, and great solace he found in fighting over again with The Counsellor the battles of the few months preceding March, 1877. With an entire devotion to his leader, and a serious scorn of the "man in the White House," he asked after the health of "his Excellency the President, who lives in Gramercy Park." Something of a reader withal he was; and Mrs. Thornton's hopeless application for a book, during the reign of the fog, elicited quite a library from the upper berth of his state-room —odd volumes of Shakespeare, Byron, Tyndall, Draper's *Conflict of Religion and Science*, Dickens, and Lever.

"We haven't got rid of that pest yet," said the chief, at a moment of general rejoicing over the sun; "unless the wind changes, it will be down on us again. Look at that fog-bank over there."

To the eastward the white column was indeed drawing near again, and there a beautiful spectacle presented itself of a ship's tops shining in the sun while all the rest was veiled in low-lying mist. The fog settled again, thicker than before, the engine slowed, and the captain announced he should go no farther. "You will spend your Fourth on board," he remarked, with grim pleasantry—a prospect rather refreshing than otherwise to passengers flying from the exuberant patriotism of a great city, though, it must be confessed, the surroundings of that narrow and often crowded channel in Nantucket Shoals were not the most desirable for a protracted sojourn in a fog. The deafening and incessant steam-pipe overhead, and warning notes from light-ships, now made the situation more depressing than before. They seemed to be set apart from the rest of the universe, to be hovering in a new world of nebulæ, through which nothing but sound could come ever to them. But that coquettish curtain arose again presently, and again the ship gave one of her glad bounds forward. Only for a moment; down it fell once more; and a heedless schooner sheering off and shooting aside just then, as she came unheralded out of the fog-bank full upon the bows of their steamer, gave them a thrill, with sense of great danger escaped.

"We have to do the looking out for these schooners," said one of the mates; "and when they don't blow their horns, and by their own fault run into us, we are called on to pay damages all the same."

The last of the line of light-ships in Nantucket Shoals marks the end of the narrow channel, through which mariners steer cautiously, until deep water and the broad swell of the Atlantic invite them to sail on fearlessly and fast. These light-ships, fully manned, and anchored from point to point, provide various signals of warning by whistle or bell so different that no one can be mistaken for any other. In the great gales of winter they sometimes break from their moorings, and go cruising down the coast, before making head against the storm.

The last of these light-ships, *Polycripp* by name, announced herself to our travellers by a sound issuing from the encompassing pillar of cloud so inexpressibly mournful and harrowing to the susceptible spirit, that the children, struck with mortal fear, rushed precipitately to the shelter of parental arms, and hid their heads, crying, "Oh, papa! suppose it should be the sea-serpent!" "The Sea-Serpent" *Polycripp* was forthwith dubbed, and no persuasions could induce one of the youngsters to desert his rock of safety until quite out of hearing of that awful wailing sound. All that could be seen of little Frank, not dangling legs or a very brief kilt petticoat, was a mass of golden curls blown across a rosy cheek and over the neck where his sturdy arms were tightly locked.

In memory of *Polycripp*, Erskine made a sketch in water-colors of the sea-serpent, fearfully and wonderfully imagined, riding at ease upon gigantic billows, and breathing on a bar of music the notes of his horrible chant. The small voyager was henceforth fully persuaded that with his own eyes he actually saw the original of the picture, and it had for him ever after a baleful fascination.

"The wind is veering, we are through the Shoals, and you are out of jail now," was the captain's cheerful announcement, as at last he came below to take a mouthful of dinner long deferred.

"O blessed west wind, that springs up to banish our foe!" cried Amy. "O stern and rock-bound coast of Massachusetts!"—("which is here all a level beach of fine sand," interpolated her brother-in-law)—"how beautiful you look, with the last wreath of mist vanishing under a glorious afternoon sun!" And now picture them, ye sweltering denizens of the workaday world, to whom also this delight is possible. They are sitting, a happy group, on the broad deck, wrapped in plaids—the breeze is stiff and cool from the wide Atlantic. The good ship, released from her curb, fairly bounds forward like a thorough-bred steed. The white surface of the sea breaks up in crests of foam. Sails are set, and wind and steam speed them swiftly towards the beacon held out on the crooked finger of Cape Cod. And ever and again, mingled with the pure smell of the salt waves, comes a whiff from the shore scented with the freshly-cut grass; all New England is making hay to-day.

And thus it is through all the lovely afternoon, and until evening closes in, when the little ones fall asleep the moment their tired, busy heads touch the pillows—no cradle-song required save the constant lapping of the sea against the flanks of the ship. In the waning sunlight they had looked better, brighter, stronger, than for weeks before. They had eaten as voraciously as young birds. Their faces had grown brown as berries, and their spirits were exhausting.

Those left on deck experienced now an hour—was it? or two, or three?—altogether delightful, and worth all the anxiety aroused by all the fogs that could have gone before. Leaving Cape Cod behind, they swiftly crossed the dancing waters of Massachusetts Bay, allured by the at first distant speck of brightness from Boston Light, that deepened and broadened into a pathway of glory leading them into the harbor. Our travellers paced the deck as tireless as the two mute shapes on the forward watch who crossed and recrossed continually from starboard to port, from port to starboard—the only other moving things visible under the black silhouette of the rigging against the starry sky. Grace seized her husband's arm and bore him away in triumph. Sometimes they dreamily lingered in the stern of the vessel, watching her track in the phosphorescent waves; then they were seized with a fit of diligent pedestrianism, stirring all the blood within their veins; then they relapsed again, and, like Mr. Wegg, "dropped into poetry," in a friendly way. They were surprised at their own eloquence, so many similes, poetical situations, and flowers of fancy came to the lips. It was really a tourney of lofty sentiment; and when the moon showed forth, and the harbor lights began to gather, as they threaded their way past one after another anchored and motionless vessel, and the far-away gleams from the shore increased in number, Grace heaved a sigh born of regret. "We are almost in. This has been too lovely for anything. But there is one great mistake: it ought to have been a honeymoon," she whispered, clinging to her husband's arm. "You are just ten years too late with·your suggestion," she was answered, politely; "but I'll remember it next time, darling."

The spell was broken. Not all the charms of sea and sky, not even the elevating reflection that they had now reached the very Hub of the Universe, could keep her on deck after that. She was "awfully sleepy;" had "been so for a long, long time;" wondered "why Amy had taken herself away with Mr. Erskine, when it was so much more jolly all together;" and "must and would go in."

Perhaps if you had questioned Erskine, he would have avowed a decided preference for being left to himself, to indulge the haunting memories he loved to conjure up. But a man would have been a churl to resist the bright and hearty, almost boyish, comradeship of Amy North, who was a desperate walker, and had not an ounce of superfluous sentiment in her composition. Erskine found himself happily exercised out of his melancholy, and also out of breath, when Miss North reluctantly followed her sister into the cabin.

IV

THEY had resolved to remain on board rather than disturb the happy little dreamers in the nursery state-room. It was midnight when the good ship touched her Boston dock, and a sound night's rest brought Grace to five o'clock in the morning of the Fourth of July, when she awoke to listen to a monotonous voice counting out thousands of Long Island cabbages, consigned, as part of the ship's cargo, by New York to æsthetic Boston folk.

Unable to sleep, she, with the eldest of her lads, reflecting that years might probably elapse before another opportunity to view the habitable globe at that hour should occur, determined to make the most of her impressions. They got ashore from a slippery rope-ladder by the aid of a kindly boatswain, and wandered around the docks and adjacent streets — all very unlike New York. There was no commotion or crowd; there were many queer old buildings, some of them with walls slated downward, and steep wooden roofs. Everything was clean and practicable for a lady's feet, and a general air of antique respectability pervaded the quarter. A strong flavor of salt characterized the whole neighborhood. Everything was of the sea, or for the use of men that go down to it in ships. The docks themselves, the outgoing and incoming ships, had an endless charm for the little lad. He speculated upon the ports whither these vessels would sail, with a fatal precision in geography, latitude and longitude, exports and imports, that put his mother's rustier memory to the blush.

"Mamma, I can't exactly remember what countries the Lesser Antilles belong to; can you?" he said, musingly, when, to her great relief, his attention became suddenly distracted to the stand of a cherry-woman close by, who dealt also in gingerbread and torpedoes.

Torpedoes! This brought her back to the fact of the Fourth of July, and aroused in her a desire to get out of the Cradle of Liberty as rapidly as possible.

"We will go to the Parker House for breakfast, Frank," she said, returning to arouse the occupant of state-room No. —. "Then we can take our time about going aboard the other ship."

"The fact is," said guilty Frank, who had gone to sleep in full consciousness of his blunder, "there's no other ship; at least, she does not sail till to-morrow afternoon. I ought to have found that out before, but I didn't. I'm awfully sorry, Grace, indeed."

"And my poor children are to spend a day — no, two days and a night — at a hot hotel in town!" Mrs. Thornton said, with awful calm. "I shouldn't be a bit surprised if it were to kill the Baby, Frank. Poor little drooping thing!"

At this moment arose from the adjoining state-room a joyful uproar. A contraband load of torpedoes had been introduced to the awakening cherubs by their older brother, and despite the remonstrances of nurse, all three of them were engaged in wildly hurling the offensive missiles wherever they would strike. Loudest among the war-cries of these night-gowned conspirators arose the delighted squeal of Baby.

"We will take train to Portland," the Counsellor said, taking advantage of a reluctant smile.

"Oh, very well," said his wife, with a resigned look. "Only, if we had known it in time, we might have stopped over with the Rutledges in Brookline—a visit I have so long promised to make."

"Yes, and have given their new baby the whooping-cough—that dreadful malady now preying upon our enfeebled ranks."

They had left the good ship ere long, and were off to the Eastern Railway station, where jostling, perspiring throngs of eager holiday folk already pouring into every train made them think tenderly of the quiet scenes of yesterday. Securing seats in a car, they checked their many trunks, their baby carriage, and their tubs, disposed of their numerous parcels in the racks, and instantly all that was picturesque in their journey had departed. The Blessed Baby, from a winsome brown-eyed water sprite became a mere mortal infant, howling even at that early hour of the day, with heat and weariness. The golden-haired traveller, aged four and a half, who had, at sea, bewitched admiring eyes with bright looks and countless vagaries, now visited the company with a public outburst of whooping-cough, scattering their fellow-voyagers from the adjacent seats. Thornton and Erskine retired into another car, with a feeble attempt to look as if they had nothing to do with the temporary centre of disturbance.

Many a book has been condemned as a consequence of sleepless nights, shooting corns, or indigestion falling to the lot of the reviewer. More than one traveller has set the seal of general condemnation on the town where he has been ill-lodged, ill-fed, or ill-attended, without regard to its actual merit. A sense of justice, therefore, blots forever from this page the beautiful city of Portland, whose commanding position, stately homes, and wide elm-arched streets deserve more than our travellers, groaning under the recollection of their stop at a great, pretentious, badly-kept hotel, are willing to concede in praise.

"Impossible to stay here twenty hours more to meet the *Lewiston*," The Counsellor said, woe-begone.

"Let us go — anyhow, anywhere," Grace and Amy said, imploringly; and they boarded a midday train for Rockland.

A good-natured jog-trot old train it proved to be, that began by waiting in the hot station until, like an ogre, it had gorged itself with babies; then, after running a little way, stopped so long (without any visible reason) that The Counsellor

and Erskine got out and wiled away the time by
gathering bunches of daisies, at which the town-
bred children clapped their hands with delight,
and every straw-hat in the party was speedily
enriched with a wreath. In and out passed hard-
featured, shuffling, brown-faced men and women,
recognizing each other with demure cordiality, and
sitting down to talk over the events that dot the
shepherd's calendar in nasal monotone rather
soothing to the ear. Our ladies found themselves
deeply interested in the fate of "Sarah Jane's
speckled hen," which "might 'a sot an' sot till she'd
'a tuk root, an' never would 'a hatched;" while
The Counsellor renounced a newspaper, and gave
his whole mind to a discussion of doctrines between two long-haired deacons on the seat behind
him—all about infant damnation and orthodoxy in
general. The car was furthermore illumined by
the presence in the flesh of no less a personage
than Mrs. Gamp—a native of Maine, off duty, so
voluble in her confidences to all in ear-shot that
none could remain in ignorance of her affairs, or
escape the information that her occupation was
plied at the Hub, "because in Boston I can make
a sight more money than here, with half the
work." Mrs. Gamp wore a bonnet and carried a
bandbox of the size and style our grandmothers
kept on remote shelves, embalmed with sprigs of
lavender; an umbrella, of course. Not more than
half a dozen teeth remained to her, and the locality of each of those was continually revealed by

a smile bestowed impartially on friends and strangers. She was a constant patron to the boy who peddled lozenges, figs, and prize candy. She imbibed oranges until the odor filled the air. She had a gossip on the seat beside her—("Perhaps, oh! perhaps it is the veritable Mrs. Harris!" whispered Amy)—to receive confidences of joys and sorrows in a ceaseless stream. Her greatest pride in life seemed to be a certain "Marier," of whom it was proudly remarked "she kep' two girls." The exact progress of the invalid she had last attended was clearly narrated with scientific precision, and her harangues went on amplifying until everybody's attention was monopolized. At one period her roving eye fell upon the Blessed Baby, whose healthy sleep on a couch of shawls, one dimpled fist near his rosy cheek, was occasionally interrupted by a cough. "I kinder mistrust that whooping-cough in a teethin' child," she remarked, cheerfully. "Ef it don't kill 'em outright, it generally goes to the brain, they say, and makes 'em weak like. Did I ever tell you the time Marier had with her young un in the whooping-cough? It jest wasted and wasted"— But at this point the mother of the Baby could bear no more, and moved to the end of the car farthest from Mrs. Gamp, whom she now knew to be a vampire.

The country they were passing through was full of quiet rural beauties, its green hill-sides covered with hay-cocks, and cows everywhere sought the shade of trees that hung their branches low over placid streams. The railway skirts the coast, and comes suddenly upon many a picturesque little village, where the deep waters lie locked in the hills. One looks in astonishment at the tall masts of vessels arising amid trees, where they have found safe harbor. "The ship-building industries seem to be looking up," said The Counsellor. "During the war these fellows, finding their occupation gone, took the field, away down in far Virginia, and made some of the best soldiers the North brought forth. See, Grace, the vertebræ of these vessels stretched upon the stocks.

> "'Ere long will we launch
> A vessel as goodly and strong and stanch
> As ever weathered a wintry sea.
> Timber of chestnut and elm and oak,
> Cedar of Maine and Georgia Pine,
> Here together shall combine.'"

At Bath their train, reduced by this time to two cars, was taken upon a boat, and ferried across the Kennebec—a noble river, fed by Moosehead Lake.

The spirits of the party began to rise, as they stood upon the rear platform of the car, and filled their lungs with fresh, exhilarating air.

When Rockland was reached, and their hearts made glad by a hotel with clean beds, clean table-cloths, and a palatable bill of fare, the tired children were left to rest, and our travellers strolled down after supper to the wharf, and stood there gazing out upon the broad expanse of the Penobscot Bay, across which, on the morrow, they were to set sail in quest of the enchanted isle of Mount Desert.

Erskine withdrew himself from the others, and climbed out upon a projection from the pier. Amy, Grace, and The Counsellor left him sitting there, and went off to explore the village. In a green yard where they were tempted to pause and look, a young woman was raking new-mown hay, occasionally tossing it over a little child, and the house wall behind her was covered with a vine of sweet old-fashioned white roses. Grace begged for a rose, and the woman, with a smile, broke off a generous cluster, and gave it to the child, who trotted to the palings and laid it in her hand.

The sun was setting; a church-bell rang for evening prayers. Erskine's unsatisfied spirit experienced a strange peace. The journey hither, in company with these kind and cheerful people, these joyous children, had been just what he required. For Amy he had conceived a very sincere regard. She made no exactions of him, or of any man. Fun, enterprise, excitement, were the breath of her nostrils. Her assumption of little mannish ways amused Erskine, where a demand for compliment would have bored him utterly. Altogether he felt better and more hopeful than he had done for months.

V

On board the little steamer *Houghton* next day our party fell in with a party of Boston pilgrims, bound to the same "haven where they fain would be." Established upon deck, with shawls and books and lunch baskets, they defied the whitecaps on Penobscot Bay that frightened quite a number of their fellow-passengers into seeking sofas down below. Amy, with her hands in the pockets of a long ulster (made by her brother-in-law's tailor, and the pride of her life), with a derby hat and a cardinal silk neck-handkerchief, walked gayly up and down.

We have no coast-line to compare in beauty and variety with that of Maine. Its jagged outline breaks up into a thousand picturesque caprices of cape and bay and headland; while islands, sown like emeralds from a sieve, are scattered in countless numbers in a field of waves. Here masses of stern gray rock arise from the seething surf; a boat's length farther on some sparkling little fiord opens through greenest meadows. Here is a cave, tinted with all the gorgeous coloring that ever dazzled Aladdin in his jewelled hall, where in crystal pools lurk a hundred living wonders of the sea, and at high tide the great waves go booming in with a voice of thunder. Close beside it is some tiny bay, tinted like "strips of the sky, fallen through from on high," and all unruffled by the wind. Under a summer sun, what voyage can be more delightful than a run in and out of the islands from Rockland to Bar Harbor? The cheery little steamer, recovering from the rude treatment of the broad Penobscot, moved soberly upon North Haven, where a row-boat was in waiting with two passengers and a trunk to be hoisted on board. After this operation they lost no time, but steamed away across the bay of Isle au Haut (pronounced "Illyhut" in the vernacular) to Deer Island, where all the population had gathered to receive an attenuated mail-bag, and a few egg boxes returned from Rockland to be refilled.

"And now," said the kindly captain, "you will see an island for every day in the year; and if you like to buy and settle hereabouts, we can sell you any one of them you take a fancy to very cheap." The eldest of Thornton's boys, with a small sum of money burning holes in his trousers pockets, pursued the captain with a thousand eager questions and presently came to his father, fired with zeal for the purchase of "that nice round island over yonder; the captain says I may have it for five dollars, or this lovely little bit of a one for seventy-five cents."

In and out between granite ledges crowned with spruce and fir, the little steamer winds her busy way; and after passing through York Narrows, with Black Island to the northward, the first view of lovely Mount Desert Island opens before them. The beacon on Bass Harbor Head stands as her sentinel; and when they draw nearer, rounding Long Ledge, the full chain of her mountains is revealed. As the day wanes, the view changes every moment, yet never wearies. Sometimes the boat, crossing a stretch where the Atlantic swell rolls in unchecked, dances like a cork on the heaving sea; then, under the shelter of an island, the water is as calm as an inland lake. Sometimes the breeze is soft and mild as an infant's breath; then suddenly there comes a change; a glacial chill borne from the bosom of a wandering iceberg descends upon them, laughed at at first, but conquering in the end, and sending them on a race to the cabin for extra wraps. Contradiction seems to be the ruling passion of Mother Nature in this region.

The first landing made at Mount Desert is Southwest Harbor, destined during the following year to be the scene of an apparition unwonted as a flamingo in a barn-yard—the mysterious ship *Cimbria* lying at anchor here for months, carrying under her German flag a horde of Russians awaiting the war-note between their master and the Queen.

All things must have an end, and this fairy voyage was drawing near its close.

Leaving Southwest Harbor one has a momentary glimpse to the northward of Somes's Sound, with a broad haven and splendid precipitous cliffs. Here came Henry Hudson in 1609, on his way south to explore the river now called after him. Here, a little later, a French colony of Jesuit fathers was attacked by the English pirate Argall; the station was plundered, and the godly priests murdered under the shadow of the cross they had so triumphantly planted on the rock with chants of thanksgiving a short time before. These worthy disciples of Christ, after many days of tossing upon angry seas, in finding themselves in the glassy waters of this tranquil sound, thought it a very paradise planted in the midst of desert rocks and had bestowed on it the original name of "Mont Désert." Their little colony, called St. Sauveur, was thus rudely destroyed; but after the lapse of nearly three centuries the memory of those good men remains, and the new church recently erected at Bar Harbor is called St. Saviour, as a reminder of their devotion.

Otter Creek was passed, and many spots whose names are dear to the heart of the faithful Mount-Deserter: Thunder Cave, the shining sands of Newport Beach, the beetling precipice of Great Head; Egg Rock with its picturesque light-house; the Anemone Cave, Schooner Head, the Spouting Horn, and the Porcupine islands, guarding the harbor over which tower mountains where one may climb through woods rich in the balsam of fir and pine trees and, emerging on the summit, look down nearly two thousand feet of precipice into the chafing ocean.

Bar Harbor was not as they had known it years ago, for the spectacle of tall hotels and "Queen

Anne" cottages made now a smart modern watering-place of what was then a quaint yellow, red, and brown tinted fisher-village on the coast.

In the harbor, side by side with fishing-smacks and Indian canoes, were gay pleasure yachts and boats, and several times a week were emptied on its pier a horde of society-seekers, alas! clad in purple and fine linen, instead of the sturdy band of young men and maidens, artists, students, professors, who would be boys again, who in earlier days wore stout shoes, and swore to dress like tramps, and dwell like gods together through long days of glorious idling in this crystal atmosphere.

The fatal tide of fashion had set that way, and having given vent to the customary Jeremiad of aboriginal visitors to Mount Desert, our travellers found it proper to admit that there were a great many consolations left under the present state of things.

"Erskine, you had better go ashore cautiously," said The Counsellor, as the little steamer touched her pier. "Ten to one there will be two rival leaders of picnic parties waiting to capture you, and bear you off in a buckboard to eat hard-boiled eggs and dismember cold chickens upon the rocks."

For once, however, this common fate was escaped, and the new-comers were only showered with cordial greetings from the picturesque groups assembled to see that great event, the arrival of the boat. Take it all in all, Bar Harbor is such an amazingly affectionate place. One grows rapturous on its wharf over friends whom one has failed to see for months, even years, in town. Snubs are forgiven, feuds are forgotten, desperate friendships are created in a breath, in this atmosphere of universal good-fellowship.

It need not be said that Miss Amy North was in her element at Mount Desert. In a moment her attached family beheld her submerged in the embraces of five particular friends among the girls, four of whom wore brilliant red petticoats and flourished Turkey red parasols.

VI

THE COUNSELLOR and his party, or Erskine and his friends, in whatever way you prefer to regard them, found that their telegrams had preceded them to some effect. Amy declared it was due to the remembrance of their attractions upon a former visit—Thornton, to everybody's fear of whooping-cough—that mine host had quartered them in the vacant rooms of a cottage sufficiently far from the madding crowd to breathe in freedom, yet near enough to become, in the Maine vernacular, "mealers," *i.e.*, go back and forth to the Rodick House for their meals.

Erskine announced that he was lodged like a prince, in a quaint little ship's cabin of a room, with floor painted green, and sunflowers and hollyhocks looking in at his window, barring the slight inconvenience of a snoring neighbor in the adjoining room, of whom it was certified by his landlady that he would not fail to leave in Monday's boat.

At breakfast next day at the Rodick their repast was continually interrupted by people who came into the great dining-room, took places, looked over at their table, looked again, as if, like Mr. Twemlow they were not quite sure whether these were indeed their dearest friends or not; then, abandoning uncertainty, descended upon the last arrivals with effusive welcome.

In this dining-room of the Rodick were then assembled representatives of all parts of the country. The F. F.'s of Boston and the F. F.'s of Virginia forgot their mutual slight unpleasantness of a few years gone by, and affiliated on the ground of common superiority to the mass of Americans not endowed like themselves with *sangre azul.* New York compared notes with Cleveland and Chicago, willing to credit them with "a certain kind of progressiveness, no doubt," but profoundly pitying them for being situated so far from the radius of her enlightening beam.

All the younger ladies were attired in short costumes, with a manifest determination towards the picturesque. "I don't care about the becomingness of it," said, to her dress-maker, a New York girl bound for Mount Desert; "but you *must* make me effective against a rock!"

Two marked peculiarities were to be noted in

the charming creatures who frequented the Eastern Eden. One was a reckless disregard of the ordinary rules for the preservation of complexion, a rich tawny brown there being as much a standard of beauty as in the Marquesas; another, the most delightful liberality in the display of stockings, which, with high-heeled slippers and sparkling buckles, were scattered over the Rodick veranda like poppies in a field.

Upon this long veranda a dress parade was held three times a day. After every meal people rallied there to plan excursions, lay out routes, discuss weather, abjure fogs, exchange novels, eat chocolate bonbons, and compare crewel-work. Truth to tell, Kensington embroidery, after a brief devotion to the æsthetic bulrush, languished in the face of yacht parties, buckboard parties, catamaran parties, and, most popular of all, those parties where two are company and three are trumpery—in the frail limitation of a birch-bark canoe.

Erskine found himself caught up and whirled away in abundant schemes mapped out for his entertainment by his friends, old and new.

Thornton's prophecy came speedily to pass. On the afternoon following their arrival they were captured, stowed in a buckboard — the Mount Desert equipage *par excellence* — and borne to a distant cliff beside the sounding sea, each man in charge of an especial keeper. Erskine thought that he might have found enjoyment more keen than in being wedged three on a seat with people from the four quarters of the globe whom he never saw before, to be driven through blinding dust, the horses going uphill and down dale at a steady gallop.

It is the correct amusement at Mount Desert to sing, while at this rate of speed, glees, catches, and choruses—a custom honorable in its antiquity, no doubt, but occasionally falling short of full effect from the preponderance of strong bass voices and shrill sopranos, as well as the rigid determination of those who never sang before to open their mouths and make a noise to add to the general hilarity. The unfortunate composer of that popular maritime ballad "Nancy Lee," should have spent a summer at Bar Harbor, in order to make him rue the day and hour when he gave it to the world.

When they reached Otter Cliffs, a glorious battlement of sea-worn, storm-riven rock, Erskine's young woman was discovered to be indispensable to the compounding of lobster salad, so he availed himself of brief freedom to clamber down nearer to the water and observe at leisure the picturesque scene.

To Amy North's portion had fallen the especial glory of the party—a young Englishman passing a few days at Mount Desert on his way to Nova Scotia.

The Honorable Cecil Clive had a fine aquiline profile, wore irreproachable knickerbockers, and divided his other interests in life with incessant contemplation of his own substantial legs, cased in woollen hose and heavy calf-skin shoes.

"I suppose you visited New York," Amy was saying, after a protracted pause.

"Oh yes, of course," said the Honorable Cecil. "Fancy not stoppin' in New York, now! And, I say, there's a capital fellow there for stoppin' teeth— whats-his-name, you know. I went to him every day I was there; upon my soul I did. He's an awfully keen fellow on teeth, now, isn't he?"

Amy shot a mischievous *œillade* towards Thornton with an expression from which he inferred that she was enjoying herself with exhilaration, and that no power on earth would detain her other than the natural sense of triumph in having appropriated the Honorable Cecil from the very grasp of "My Lady Disdain," as they called Mrs. Ketchum from New York.

This lady having, with her two pretty inane daughters, once been presented at Queen Victoria's court, and visited two or three English country houses, had conceived the idea of becoming a sort of self-constituted duchess in New York society. A foreigner of distinction or of title fell into her hands upon his arrival as naturally as an October apple gravitates towards the earth. A brace of English lordlings had even been recently consigned to her care by their respective mammas, with the polite injunction to keep them from the snares of American match-makers—a request rigidly, though not intentionally (so ill-natured people said), complied with. It may be, then, readily imagined that this American fairy godmother of the English aristocracy had every reason to resent interference with the Honorable Cecil, her rightful property.

Mrs. Ketchum sat upon the rocks, with discontent written on every line of her countenance, supported on either side by the pretty daughters, who had hung fire at Mount Desert in consequence of their inability to comprehend "these odd American ways." Mrs. Ketchum refused to be comforted even by the attendance of that great arbiter of fashion Mr. Philip Daly, who was spending a week at Bar Harbor before adjourning to Newport, "just to see what people find to like in it, by Jove!"

It was apparent that Mr. Philip Daly's principle in life resembled that of Dickens's hero, who would rather be knocked down by a gentleman than picked up by a cad. His conversation with Mrs. Ketchum consisted mainly of warmed-over reminiscences of their respective English experiences, in discussion as to whether it was Lord Partington's wife's sister or his half-sister who had just eloped with young Plantagenet Grenville.

My Lady Disdain only consented to relax into a wan sort of a smile when Mr. Daly disclosed to her an entirely new anecdote, just received, about Mrs. Langtry and the Prince of Wales.

Higher up on the cliff sat Mrs. Hazelhurst, an aristocratic dame of noble Dutch stock, whose wont it was to "sit upon thrones in a purple sublimity," and repress the "audacity of people in trade, my dear, aspiring to lead in New York society." Mrs.

Hazelhurst considered it her duty to draw the line somewhere, and she drew it at Mrs. Ketchum.

Mrs. Hazelhurst was in close conversation with Grace Thornton about some one of their mutual "fads." Mrs. Thornton was a typical young New York matron, and the possession of a husband and a pretty little house overflowing with bric-à-brac and babies, did not prevent her embarking in every kind of enterprise, social, philanthropic, pious, or patriotic.

Mrs. Thornton had, at home a little blue and white cretonne morning-room, all over crooks and Cupids, where in one corner was placed a davenport, severely dedicated to public works. Here she sat, amid piles of reports and other documents, writing innumerable little notes, and overhauling her visiting list in the intervals of drawing up the minutes of her last meeting with a crimson feather pen.

Mrs. Hazelhurst was the president of the Anti-Cassowary Sisters of Timbuctoo. Mrs. Thornton was secretary of the Alb Association and Chasuble Club. Both ladies patronized sewing societies, hospitals, amateur theatricals flannel-petticoat guilds, and Orthopœdic bazars at Delmonico's.

"Mon Dieu, madame!" said a young Frenchman to Mrs. Thornton one season, "I have come to think that your *gracieuses* American ladies have a veritable mania for good works. If I escape from a salon where there are rose-colored and blue tickets for sale, I call upon a charming person who excuses herself to attend a committee or to visit an asylum for blind or lunatics."

In conference with these two ladies was Mr. Peters, a very round, blond, and rosy personage, whom nature meant for a good-natured kindly diner-out, but who persisted in adopting a mournful and poetic rôle. His especial weakness or gift was for the construction of neatly turned essays upon the character of deceased friends. Irreverent girls like Amy North called poor Mr. Peters "The Ghoul," and men said of him that it added new terrors to death to know that Peters would inevitably write your obituary for publication in the *E———g P——t*.

The Counsellor, rejoicing in the good-fortune of his wife and sister, had taken possession of a lovely little Philadelphia girl, with cheeks like wild roses blooming at the bottom of a scoop straw-hat, according to an agreement with Grace that he might flirt as much as he pleased at Mount Desert.

A pair of sisters, Louisiana creoles, with brilliant mobile faces, lips of pomegranate, and complexions that resembled the white of a camellia petal, were resting upon a crimson rug from their unusual labors in ascending the steep cliff, and at their feet were stretched a bevy of Harvard men, whom these soft Southern beauties had completely carried by storm.

Two Boston ladies, themselves resembling sketches by Du Maurier, had brought their water-colors, and were diligently at work, ambitious to catch an especial point of view under the supervision of the famous artist Shorterfeldt, whom all the amateurs were following—"a very long way after," as *Punch* would say.

The "Baltimore delegation" of pretty, slender girls, with irresistibly cordial ways, had undertaken to build a fire of drift-wood, whose pale blue column of smoke arose under the shoulder of a huge rock. Into their service they had impressed a number of cavaliers, among them no less a star than the youthful Knickerbocker Mr. Percy De Witt, whose dear little hands were assuredly more at home in wielding a fan to conduct the Cotillon than in the Caliban service of fetching heavy logs.

Everywhere echoes of cheerful laughter from merry maidens smote the ear. One sees the Bar Harbor colony out in force at such a festival as this.

Erskine was out of tune with gayety, and by no one of these attractive groups did he care to linger long. He strayed down to the verge of the chafing sea, and walked idly up the coast. Sometimes he crossed a wall of ragged rocks upon which the long roll of the Atlantic spent its force. Beyond, a forest of leaves, layer upon layer of every conceivable shade of green, wooed the foot to follow where the eye had plunged. Again, he passed a stretch of beach, green and glittering with the spines of countless sea-urchins, powdered by the action of the waves. Then came an inlet, where the surf swirled up between two black and frowning walls. Next, a tiny path through a bit of fern pasture, all embedded in moss and red berries, and overhung with tangled boughs of birch. And so, with errant footsteps, on and on, until he came suddenly out again upon a stretch of unimpeded coast, and stood upon a jutting point of rocks.

There, full in his view, across an intervening bay, he saw an archway of stone, gorgeous with prismatic hues, where at certain conditions of the tide a single boat might float in on the wave, and rest its keel upon a bit of pebbly beach. Behind it rose a beetling crag to shut off all retreat, and a little stream of water, crystal clear, came stealing down between tufts of harebells growing where no hand could reach. Here, in this cool recess, might one retire to gaze out upon the wide panorama of islands rising from a sapphire sea; and here, like a picture set in a frame, he saw a lady stand.

Erskine's breath grew short, and a dimness passed before his eyes. It was none other than Rosalie Gray. It was evident that she had rowed herself into the cavern, and found it a much more difficult matter to return. The waves were dashing in upon her feet, and the little cockle-shell of a boat was beating and grinding on the rocks in utter rebellion against her attempt to bring it into subjection with a line or oar.

One moment Erskine gave to the luxury of gazing upon her unobserved. She was more beautiful, he thought, in the dark blue boating dress, with the fish-woman's tunic and coarse straw-hat, than in all the bravery of silk attire and gems. The lines of her figure, the poise of her head, were here revealed in a new phase, that seemed in some way to bring her more down to his level than before. In her belt she wore with careless grace a large knot of the ox-eyed daisies just then starring every field upon the island, another in her hat.

"I beg your pardon—mayn't I help you?" Erskine hailed her. As she turned and saw him the flush in her cheek deepened perceptibly. In a moment's time he was scrambling over the slippery rocks regardless of appearances, and torn, rough, and breathless, presented himself before her.

His first task was to capture the boat, and, walking in water to his knees, hold it with a firm grasp until the passenger was safely stowed within.

"Now keep your oars shipped for a moment, please, and here goes;" and with a mighty push Erskine shot the little craft far out beyond the passage-way, but simultaneously lost his footing, and plunged headlong into deep water after it.

Before Mrs. Gray had time to realize her dismay he was up again, and scaling the rocks as he dashed the brine away, vowed that he would walk back to the party, and beg for hot coffee and a wrap.

"It is absolutely nothing, I assure you," he said, as she rowed up to his side. "Who would count a wetting in sea-water like this? though I must confess it has a sting of cold, as if the splinter from an iceberg had touched me passing by. It is rather a downfall to my pride, however, to appear before you in such a way."

"You are too good, to make light of it. Thanks again," Rosalie said, every trace of reserve departing from her manner. "I am more than ashamed of myself to have been the cause of such an accident. It is quite impossible for you to think of returning to your party. They will have left The Cliffs probably, and it is a great way off. I beg—I insist that you come into my boat, take this rug, and let me row you home."

"Everything but that," Erskine said, acquiescing, with a smile. "Pray be compassionate, and don't bring me to shame by making an invalid of me. I bargain for the oars myself."

What between the active exertion of a long pull and the astonishing excitement of the situation, he had nothing to fear from lack of circulation of the blood. Like a draught of wine was the delicious look of sympathy she turned upon him. He almost wished that he might have struck his head upon a submerged rock, in order to pose a little, and win still more of these anxious womanly glances. There was nothing left of the imperial ball-room belle; she was dreamy and almost shy.

Nothing passed between them in reference to their former meetings. In society one recognizes that there are a great many things convenient to forget, and that almost everybody has a time when it is best to rub out bad marks and begin over again. Mrs. Gray may have murmured, "I met you at the Patriarchs' last winter, I believe?" and Erskine may have answered, "Yes—ah, certainly.

I think I was indebted to my friend A—— for the pleasure ;" but neither one betrayed any profounder emotion.

When Perseus proceeded to land Andromeda at a floating-dock, and to assist her up the steep stairway, she waited until they were out of hearing of the ring of lounging boatmen, and turning, offered him her slim white hand.

"Mr. Erskine," she said, for the first time pronouncing his name, "let me thank you again, the more heartily because I have to ask your pardon for another offence."

It did not occur to Erskine to demand for what just then. His blood was thrilling in his veins. He looked after her stately figure as she walked away, without even knowing if they should meet again.

VII

They did meet again, early and oft, after the friendly Mount Desert fashion. "Better a fortnight of Mount Desert that a cycle in New York," say enthusiasts in the art of love-making. It is a very dispensary of opportunities.

Mrs. Gray was stopping with her aunt — a delightful old lady with pretty white crimped hair, who did endless bands of crewel-work — and that lady's husband, Mr. Carson, at a cottage at some distance from the centre of gayety, the Rodick House. Although Mrs. Gaspar Gray habitually declined picnics and large excursion parties, she was more accessible to her friends here than in town.

The day after his adventure Erskine was sauntering listlessly up and down the board walk in the chief street with his hands stuck in his tweed pockets, utterly unconscious of the siren glances bestowed on him by numbers of pretty girls lounging on verandas or steps, under scarlet or blue umbrellas, with pretty little feet coquettishly displayed before them. It was this provoking indifference of Mr. Erskine's, the young ladies agreed, that made him so very desirable. Poor, good-natured Tom Elliott, who spent his time in everybody's service, whose life was one struggle "to get up something new" for the diversion of society, wandered up and down like Noah's weary dove, vainly seeking a resting-place beside some of these indifferent fair ones. He compromised at last upon a promenade with Miss Amaryllis Glover, who had weathered dear knows how many summers at Mount Desert, and had gone to so many picnics in her day that one trembles at the thought of computing the number of sandwiches she must have consumed, not to mention Albert biscuits and sardines.

Not until Amy North came down the Rodick steps — a fact noted promptly by several curious damsels, and put on record by old Mrs. Delancey, the picket-guard of the Rodick House, who was always on duty by the hall door, armed with her knitting-pins — did Mr. Erskine arouse from his reverie and join her with a smile. The fact was, he had been guilty of the unconscionable weakness of hanging round the principal thoroughfare solely with a view to catching a possible glimpse of Mrs. Gray, or of gaining some insight into her movements for the day.

So far, he had entirely failed, and the spectacle of Amy North in her boating dress was sufficiently consolatory to make him feel that a morning spent with this "dear charmer" might atone for the absence of "t'other." Amy's light figure and springy grace of motion were best seen in her jaunty sailor's suit of blue and white. Her little tarpaulin hat set upon the golden braids, and the short "banged" hair in front, gave her a childish look, sustained by the fearless wide-open blue eyes looking out of a somewhat sun-kissed dimpled little face.

"May I go with you, my pretty maid?" Erskine said to her.

"If you choose to come out in the canoe with me and my own Indian, and will promise not to touch the paddle. I am quite an expert."

"If you will take me in exchange for your own Indian," he said. "I am eminently cautious and conservative."

"I don't know that that is an especial recommendation to me," Amy said, with her light-hearted laugh. "But wait here a moment, please, while I run back to the house for my scarlet silk neck-handkerchief. I would do you discredit without my bit of color in the canoe."

As she left him, a lady passed Erskine and walked into a village shop, which contained everything imaginable in addition to the daily mail to Bar Harbor.

It was Rosalie Gray, and he was by her side as her foot touched the threshold.

"Good-morning," Erskine said, with a strange lack of self-possession. "I have been watching for you all the morning. I did not exactly like to present myself at your quarters, and I wanted to know if—if you are quite well to-day."

"I should rather ask you that question, Mr. Erskine, for you were the principal sufferer," she said, lightly, and looking him in the eyes, with the indefinable airy confidence of a woman of the world.

"Oh, if you mean my wet clothes, that is nothing. May I—might I walk home with you this morning?" he went on, feeling more and more at a disadvantage.

At that moment Amy came running out upon the walk, ready for their jaunt, and summoned him as unceremoniously as if she were a boy and he a school-fellow.

Mrs. Gray's face wore an amused look as she offered him her hand.

"Another time," she said, in her quiet voice. "Let me wish you, instead, a pleasant paddle and better luck than befell you in my service."

"Do you row much? Do you care for a canoe? May I take you out to-morrow?" Erskine said, with a profound rebellion against the trick Fate was playing him.

"Come to my cottage to-morrow morning about eleven, and we may talk it over. One never can promise anything too surely at Mount Desert. There are fogs, you know, and other interruptions. Pray don't let me keep you a moment longer from that charming young lady now."

There was nothing left about her of the heavenly softness of the day before. Her manner was cool, though sufficiently cordial, easy, bright, and careless. Erskine, who had been for hours hungering for another one of those looks from her soft dark eyes, went back to Amy, consumed with disappointment.

"So that is Mrs. Gaspar Gray," Amy said, with a girl's admiring curiosity. "I did not know she was here, or that you knew her. I think she is too splendid for anything; but that sort of a woman always makes me feel as if my gown doesn't fit, or the buttons are off my boots, or as if I have large red hands, and don't know how to do my hair."

Erskine thought it would be difficult for this little town-bred creature to look other than she was—fine and fair to see. Her unaffected admiration of his divinity aroused in him for her a new warmth of friendship. He resolved that he would bring these two women together, as men often do, not always with success. Hope springing eternal pointed him to the morrow when he was bidden to Rosalie's cottage, and his spirits rose. They walked down to the point of embarkation, chatting merrily, and Amy, hailing *her* Indian (otherwise the one chartered by Mr. Thornton for especial attendance upon the whims of his enterprising young sister-in-law), their canoe was run up beside a float and they were stowed within. The Indian was dismissed, but Erskine received orders to take his ease, reclining luxuriously, while Amy paddled their tiny craft across the "glassy, cool, translucent wave."

"I feel like a Moslem saint reclining in paradise," Erskine said, dreamily, as they floated in from the sun-glare to the haven of a shaded little bay so noiselessly that they scarce disturbed a legion of bright fishes darting underneath their keel.

"If Moslem saints have their noses burned to a bright red, then you certainly resemble one," said his skipper. "This is chief of the drawbacks to romance upon the water at Mount Desert. See, Mr. Erskine, how clear the water is over this shallow, and how the bottom shines like silver near the shore."

They gazed down in fascinated silence through the amber veil upon the under-world. There, over sunken rocks, matted with olive-tinted kelp, swaying lazily in the current, passed and repassed the busy workers of submarine commerce, jostling, struggling, and devouring each other quite as they do up above.

"Let us go ashore here," said Amy. "I am filled with a desire to explore the wooded sides of this Porcupine."

"Let us rather seek a shady nook, and loaf," Erskine said. "We have had 'enough of action and of motion we.'"

"*We!*" said Amy, scornfully. "I should like to be told how large a share of it has fallen to you. But, as Grace says, there is nothing so easy to spoil as men, and you shall be made to work your passage back, I promise you."

She consented to indulge his idleness, after all, and they found shelter beneath a downward sweeping branch, where Erskine stretched himself at half length upon a carpet of pine-needles, and looked up into her face.

Amy took his straw hat and decorated it with a cavalier's plume of ferns growing out of a cleft in the rocks near by.

"Now you are my knight," she said, conferring it upon him with a fantastic little gesture.

Erskine thought it not unnatural that he should respond to this by taking her hand in his and kissing it with a courtly grace. At the very moment chosen for the exploit another canoe shot across the water at their feet, and Rosalie Gray and the Indian who propelled it had the full benefit of this pretty pastime.

The Indians at Mount Desert must be rather accustomed to that kind of thing, for the present spectator looked to the full as stolid as his kind, and Mrs. Gray gave no more evidence of consciousness than did her dusky guide.

"It is just my luck, Grace," said Amy, coming into her sister's room that night in a blue cashmere dressing-robe, with her yellow locks hanging loose around her indignant little face. "I, who never did anything fast in my life—in that way, I mean—and just because Mr. Erskine kissed my hand, every bit in fun, you know, that Mrs. Gaspar Gray should be the one to come upon us! If she had only laughed, it would have been some consolation, but she barely nodded, and looked more like the Empress of—Everything—than usual. How stupid it all is! Men are great nuisances, I think. One may be happy forever, and as soon as they get mixed up with things, trouble sets in."

"Very true, dear," said the matronly Grace, heaving a sigh she thought she might venture upon without disloyalty to Frank. "But there they are, and we must make the best of them. Now let this teach you to be careful, Amy, for there never was such a place as this, and whether you flirt or whether you don't, people will be sure to suspect you."

"Then what is the use of self-denial?" was Amy's very natural inquiry, her mischievous spirit springing up.

"If you only heard the confidences that are made to me!" Grace went on, unheeding this indiscretion. "I don't know what there is about me, but I am a perfect repository of love secrets. Flirtation is in the very 'hair of the hatmosphere' at Mount Desert.

And girls, Amy, whom you would never suspect of it at home. As to the men, why, there is that nice young Grafton, in Frank's office, who met a girl coming up on the *Lewiston* from Portland, spent three days in devoting himself to her on verandas and at picnics, and proposed to her on the fourth day, before ever having seen her with her hat off. Fortunately she was already engaged to be married, he told me, for when she did appear bareheaded her forehead went so far back he was in an agony lest she should say 'yes.'"

"But what *will* Mrs. Gray think of me?" said Amy, ingrevert to her own grievance, as she wielded her ivory brush.

"Oh! I don't know," said Mrs. Thornton, with a strong desire to laugh, which she repressed from motives of decorum. "If she knows Mr. Erskine at all, she will know he did it in a brotherly kind of a way, I suppose."

Why should the unreasonable blood have mounted up to Amy's face at this? Only a woman can tell, I fancy. Perhaps Grace had some sly design of her own in throwing out this fly to catch a fish. She changed the subject by inviting Amy to go into the nursery and look at Baby—an act of worship performed by both women nightly with unfeigned faith and love.

There he lay, the monarch of their hearts, in his little cot, with golden rings of hair clinging to his moist brow, and a rosy flush upon his cheeks, resting the tired feet that all day long had trotted on the coast, and the hands relaxed from their labor of fetching and carrying sticks and stones. Beneath his pillow nurse revealed a huge pine cone, without which Baby would by no means have been induced to go to sleep, and an invalid tin soldier was just dropping out of the dimpled fist.

The other beds contained two sturdy slumberers, who, having been consigned to rest in the ordinary attitude, had gradually worked themselves around at right angles with each other, and at intervals kicked out wildly, scattering the bed-clothes far and near. Above their heads two shelves contained their museum of treasures collected during the day. Pebbles, bits of lobster shells and claws, "sea-dollars," dried starfish, the shells of sea-urchins perforated with a skill no Chinese carver on ivory could surpass, mussels, oysters overgrown with sea-weed—what was there not?

"I'm in mortal fear, ma'am, that this rubbish will begin to smell, if it don't already," said nurse, carrying her case to the highest tribunal; "but it's as much as my life is worth to touch one of the nasty things. Coaxing ain't of no use, and I'd be much obliged to you, ma'am, if you'd speak about it yourself to the young gentlemen."

Grace promised redress, but surveyed the scene with satisfaction unalloyed.

"After all, my dear," she said, as they turned away, "it does give one a better opinion of men, to think they belong to the same class with Frank and the boys, doesn't it?"

VIII

It is to be supposed that to Erskine's lot fell most of the suffering from his thoughtless act of gallantry to Amy. No one's society had power to retain him during that evening, and he spent the hours in wandering about the village in the vicinity of Rosalie's cottage home, and in keeping watch like a devotee over the casement where a light was burning. This light was, in reality, the kerosene lamp by which dear old Mrs. Carson was putting up her crimps; but what did it matter, after all?—he was just as much comforted by surveying the wrong side of the house.

At a very few minutes past eleven o'clock next day he presented himself in Rosalie's little sitting-room, to be received, as he might have expected to be, like any other morning caller.

Her surroundings, as she sat sketching a cluster of field flowers stuck in a blue china jar, were full of picturesque grace in decoration and arrangement. A few Eastern rugs and Japanese hanging screens, sketches in water-color or in charcoal, jugs, draperies, bibelots, a wicker-chair tied with knots of cardinal ribbon, a chintz-covered lounge, a bowl filled with brier roses in masses of shaded pink, books, and an easel, had transformed the homely cottage room into an artist's interior.

During the ensuing conversation not once could Erskine find a loop-hole to introduce an explanation of the island scene she had unintentionally become aware of. It was clear that she intended to exclude personalities from the range of their talk. Whatever of impulse she had exhibited to him on the occasion of his exploit at the cave was exhausted then. Her manner was courteous, though somewhat measured.

Mrs. Gaspar Gray knew too well the opening manœuvres of a suitor's campaign to expose to them any part of her own plan of defense. He felt the full charm of the well-bred woman of society in her politeness, neither flattering nor coquettish; her tact in generalizing conversation; her subtle force in putting between them a bridge of glass over which he dared not tread.

Erskine talked with her long, and with ever-increasing interest. He soon realized in some inexplicable way, that in proportion to his abandonment of the manner most expressing his real feeling, her geniality and *bienveillance* (what English word will say this for me?) increased.

She was more than a match for him in this delicate contest, and when Erskine rose to go, he felt as if he had been brushed in the face by a butterfly's wing, and none the less repelled.

"You are with the Thornton party, I understand, Mr. Erskine?" she said, as he was leaving. "I know Mrs. Thornton a little, in town, but my aunt was intimate with her mother long ago, and has charged me to seek out the daughters for her sake. The young lady—Miss North—is charming, I think. I hope they will like to come to our cottage sometimes, when they are tired of the bustle at the Rodick. This is a quiet little nook of ours for such a crowded place. It is just what I needed, and what I like. The sea is my best friend, after all, for in my boat or canoe, exploring these lovely shores, I can be most sure of the rest and solitude I seek. I can't always hope to be so fortunate, if trouble overtakes me, as to have such aid as yours. You must go, then? Thanks, so very much, for being willing to come away from all the gayety to bestow an hour on me. Don't forget to tell your friends about Mrs. Carson, and, when they come to see us, you will come with them, may I hope?"

From that day forth Erskine fell quietly into the position assigned to him by Mrs. Gray. They met frequently, but always on the same terms. He did not renew his offer to accompany her boating excursions, and in these most of her hours of daylight were spent. When he visited the cottage, Mr. and Mrs. Carson and other friends were always there. With the Thorntons and with Amy North his intimacy daily increased. Visits had passed between them and Mrs. Gray, who dazzled and delighted at least two of the family, if the third did not yield unresistingly.

The summer days slipped down the rosary of Time; every boat brought a fresh contribution of visitors to the already overcrowded island. Enough rain had fallen to lay the dust; the weather was perfect; altogether Bar Harbor was in the full swing of a prosperous season.

"It is just as if the Venus de Milo had consented to leave her cool corner of the Louvre," The Counsellor said one day, while straying with his wife and boys down the path leading to the Indian encampment, whither he was decoyed to buy "baskets and things" by those arch-conspirators.

It was a delicious stroll in the sunshine, along a grassy bluff, the harbor at their feet lying like a mirror to reflect the blue of cloudless heavens and the green shores of island and main-land, while the sails hung idle, and fishermen were resting from their early morning's toil. The Counsellor felt as if he could forgive his enemies and forget his clients so long as this glorious weather should endure.

The necessities of the path compelled them to progress in single file—a fact in itself rather annoying to the person who walks behind, especially if anything not entirely audible is said. This may have accounted for the somewhat tart accents of Mrs. Thornton's voice when she requested him to repeat his remark, begging to know to whom it might refer.

"Why, is there more than one Venus de Milo?" he answered, turning back with cheerful alacrity. "I mean, of course, that magnificent Mrs. Gray. I have sometimes suspected Erskine of being touched in her quarter, and I wish him good-luck, with all my soul, though there are some inconveniences attending the translation of a goddess from the clouds to sit behind one's soup tureen."

"You are too silly, Frank," said Grace, coming up in her impatience to thrust her hand within his arm. "Why are you so blind as not to see that Erskine is just the person for Amy? Mrs. Gray would never think of marrying again. Why should she? Look at her position. She is perfectly happy. In the first place, she is a widow—"

"Thank you for the hint," said her husband.

"—she has a house and fortune, nobody to contradict her, liberty to travel when and where she pleases, to indulge all her tastes. How stupid it is for such women to *want* to marry, when this world is so full of nice girls, and there are so few nice men!"

"With what dash does this unblushing young general unmask her batteries!" said The Counsellor.

"But, you know, darling, that Erskine has been more with Amy than with any other girl this season, and though she did not care a straw for him in the beginning, I have sometimes thought lately that she might be brought to fancy him."

"And why bring her to fancy him if he does not fancy her?" said Frank, clinching the thing in what Grace always called "that hateful manly way."
"Why try to induce a state of affairs on the hypothesis that it will all turn out as you like? By Jove! Grace, I'll tell you what I believe — you women take to match-making for the excitement of it, as gamblers take to cards."

"You are very low in your way of putting it," Mrs. Thornton said, with an air of fine scorn. "I don't suppose it makes the least difference to you that a woman's feelings may be concerned. Only, dear"—and with a sudden change of base she drew so near to him that her cheek touched his shoulder—" you are so good and kind to our darling Amy, that *if anything should come of this*, I know you won't spoil everything by talking to Mr. Erskine about goddesses and all that, or putting it into his head that he is in love with Mrs. Gray. Say you won't, Frank."

"You have revealed your weak spot, Grace. You are afraid of Mrs. Gray."

But not another word would she vouchsafe upon the subject. She became as sweet as honey dropping from the comb. They sauntered on, amid the booming of bees and the nodding of clover, the children darting into the sweet vanilla-scented grass in pursuit of butterflies, and running back with "flowers for mamma." Thornton made up his mind, like a sensible fellow, that submission to authority was a cheap price at which to purchase peace like this.

IX

AT the Indian encampment they made the usual tour from tent to tent, investing small sums in baskets delicately woven of the sweet-smelling grass growing about the fields; in bows, arrows, birch-bark canoes, lacrosse bats strung with thongs of deer leather, and much in demand by the critical small boy; in grebe or sea-gulls' breasts and wings; in skins and feather fans — until even these insatiate shoppers cried "Enough!"

At the last tent the children paused in admiration of a very stolid-looking pappoose overflowing with fat, whose mother, a handsome young squaw, with her hair bound up in a red cotton handkerchief, and — shades of Pocahontas! — clad in a black alpaca gown, with rusty knife-pleatings, had suspended him in a hammock between two trees, while she sat weaving her basket silently at the opening of her tent, overhanging the water's edge.

Impressed by the attention he received, she unstrapped the pappoose, and set him on his feet to confront the Blessed Baby of the Thornton family, who stood gazing at the small copper-colored apparition, with awe depicted on his countenance. Then, with a quick sentence or two in her own tongue, the squaw reached up, and taking down the topmost basket from a long string of them, placed it in her baby's hand with the first smile she had bestowed upon the scene, and motioned him to present it to the visitor. The harsh and unwonted sound had the unfortunate effect of reducing Thornton *minimus* to bitter tears, welling irrepressibly, and not to be stanched until he was safe within the strong shelter of his father's arms.

While Mr. Thornton was engaged in consoling his infant, and inducing it to bestow a small coin upon the unwinking and sphinx-like pappoose, the other lads were trying to investigate the interior of a small plank structure, not unlike a hen-house, built behind the tent. Out of this came sounds much exciting their curiosity.

"It must be pigs, Indian pigs," the oldest boy said, solemnly. "Please, may we look?" he asked the squaw; who nodded in her imperturbable fashion; and there, inside the pen, they saw two small boys, aged about five and eight, poking their brown fingers through the apertures, and gazing out cheerfully with their bright black eyes. Shut up here for safe-keeping and general convenience, their mamma had obviated all the usual difficulties in the matter of seasonable clothing by leaving them in the costume of our first ancestors before the fall.

"Here comes nurse for Baby," the boys announced, as that functionary, in French cap and long apron, and an expression of countenance as if she had ceased being surprised at the latitude allowed her young charges in this remote spot, came briskly down the path.

"And now, papa—please, oh, please! It is just the day for mackerel-fishing. Let us get a boat, and row over there off Bar Island. We can stop at the fish-house on the island for bait and lines. I know the nicest man there, papa. He's my particular friend, only he smells a little of fish. He will lend us lines and all. He knows everything, papa—a great deal more than you do; all about boats, and tides, and porpoises, and whales, and where the blueberries grow, and how to get birch bark off—oh! lots of things!"

"The Lilliputians have overcome Gulliver," said The Counsellor, as he found himself being dragged off to visit this Admirable Crichton of a fisherman. "Come, Grace; we will put you ashore if the sun proves too much for you."

And Grace, nothing loath, we may be sure—for her heaven on earth was in the joy of these three —followed over long strips of birch bark drying in the sun, past where the Indians were constructing their canoes, and to the water's edge. A large flat-bottomed boat was secured, Grace and her umbrella established in the stern, and they steered for the opposite shore, Frank doing the main work with one oar, and his oldest boy manfully tugging, as was his especial pride, at the other.

The boy's hero was unfortunately absent from his usual scene of duty, on a deep-sea fishing jaunt, but a substitute presented himself, and supplied all necessary apparatus, including a tin can full of chopped bits of raw herring for bait.

"Now you may land me speedily," said Grace, as this odorous object was deposited at her feet. "Put me ashore just after you round the island, please, and I will wait there cheerfully until you have caught Polycripp himself."

She made an ineffectual effort to induce her

younger boy to remain ashore with her, and seek an asylum from the sun. He refused stoutly, shaking his golden locks, and clinging to his father's arm, tenacious of this first permission to assume the coveted privileges of a big boy.

The boat glided off again out of the cool green shadows into the sunshine. Grace climbed up to the edge of the wooded hill and, half hidden in a nest of tall ferns, sat where she could look out under shelving boughs, and see it courtesying on the little waves, where they had anchored to throw out their lines.

It was one of those days in Mount Desert waters that make everything else seem tame by comparison—intoxicating in the fulness of midsummer beauty. Grace sat a while, satisfied, with

> "half-shut eyes, ever to seem
> Falling asleep, in a half-dream.

There was a sound of footsteps on the slope behind, and Rosalie Gray, with her hands full of ferns, came along the path from out the sombre boskage of the woods.

"I have been rambling over the island to fill my jars and vases," she said, with a word of greeting. "My boat is beached behind that bowlder yonder, and I have found treasures of lovely ferns. May I sit by you and rest before embarking for my homeward pull? You look so thoroughly in the spirit of the place and the day that I envy you. I think you must like, as I do, to be sometimes utterly alone."

"I try to persuade myself that I do," answered Grace, laughing; "but the last few years of my life have been so spent in dividing and subdividing my time and attention, and in doling them out to others, that I am afraid I have lost even the faculty to enjoy seclusion. I am perpetually forming plans for arriving at a period when I can cultivate my own thoughts, and the time never comes. All that I ever accomplish in this world is done in desperate rushes, as if I were behindhand for a train about to start. Sometimes I fairly long for a week, or a day, when I can sit still and rally up my scattered faculties. You have no idea, Mrs. Gray, what an undignified contrast my life presents to yours, for example."

"I have a very clear idea," said Rosalie, in a low tone, while her look expressed the "star-like sorrow of immortal eyes." "Ah, Mrs. Thornton, believe me that there is no epoch of a woman's life so infinitely sad as when she realizes that in all the world there is not one whose happiness depends on her self-sacrifice."

"Listen! listen!" said Grace, springing to her feet, as a merry shout came across the water. She saw her husband bareheaded in the boat, waving his hat towards her. The little boys were waving too, and cheering lustily, as they pointed to a fine mackerel, shining like silver, held up on the line of the proud little golden-haired fisherman in the stern. "He has caught it himself! How happy he must be, my darling one!" Grace cried, sending her blue veil fluttering towards them in response. She sat down, her face flushed with purest joy, a little ashamed of her irrepressible outburst. To her surprise, Rosalie's eyes were full of tears.

"Forgive me," Mrs. Gray said, gently; "I am weaker than I thought."

"Dear Mrs. Gray," Grace said, in her impulsive way, "you teach me how to value my blessings. Only to-day I spoke to my husband about your lot, as being the most enviable one a woman ever had."

"And yet you would not change with me!" Rosalie said, with a sad smile. "We shall be better friends, I think, henceforth. It will do me good to know you and yours, for I am very poor in friends. And that sweet little sister of yours, too. If I could, I should like to be her friend. What a blessing her fresh young companionship must be to you always!"

"I am afraid I have almost too much for my share," Grace said, stopping to think what she would be without Frank, or her boys, or Amy; which of them she could by any possibility give up; what wealth or power would make amends to her for losing these. "I am glad you like Amy, for she is a darling. She feels for you that sort of championing admiration a girl sometimes cherishes in secret for a woman older and more brilliant than herself. Dear little Amy! We are orphans, as you know, and her happiness is very near to me."

"And there is no claim on her still nearer?" said

Rosalie, turning aside to strip a birch bough of its leaves. " You probably know what is the common report here of her engagement with our friend Mr. Erskine. Surely you could not do more wisely than commit her happiness to the keeping of a man like that ?"

Grace started and, with her husband's hint still fresh in her memory, looked narrowly at Mrs. Gray; but there was no indication of anything more than delicate womanly solicitude, and she breathed a sigh of positive relief.

" If I were to tell you how much I had set my heart on the reality of that, you would laugh at me, probably, as Frank does. I have no reason to believe in it—as yet; that is the candid truth; but I know they have been together constantly, and I have sometimes thought—on Amy's side—I beg your pardon, Mrs. Gray, and Amy's too, for discussing her affairs in this way. I am sure I don't know what tempted me;" and Grace recovered herself, with a feeling of actual guilt.

" Shall I tell you what tempted you?" Rosalie said, taking her hand, and speaking with irresistible simplicity. " Was it not because you felt that the name and maidenly reserve of a young girl are as safe in my hands as if I were her sister or her mother? Be sure now that you can trust me, and rely on me."

The fishing-boat touched shore, and shrill young voices filled the air with twittering, like early birds of spring. Grace was borne away in triumph, to be installed amid piles of silver-bellied mackerel, three of them claimed as the especial spoil of her little sunburned rogue.

Rosalie was left alone. Soon she was seated in her boat, and pulling homeward with that long light stroke at once the envy and admiration of every woman on the island.

X

THE season at Mount Desert is comparatively short, and the earliest days of autumn find the hotels sadly thinned of guests. By the middle of September, the most beautiful part of the year in that region, almost every one has vanished.

Some of our friends lingered on after the close of August. Frank Thornton, having gone back to town for an interval of solitary work, finding it more than he could bear, had returned to Bar Harbor to take possession of his family. They, with Amy North, were to leave in a few days.

Mrs. Gray and the Carsons, making up their minds that no place would suit them half so well until they should go to the Berkshire hills, had determined to remain.

Erskine, whose first visit to Bar Harbor had lasted much longer than originally intended, had gone back finally to New York, and now reappeared upon the scene, to be consigned with remarkable unanimity of public voice to the custody of Miss North. That he would accompany the party upon their return was a foregone conclusion. Amy's friends among the girls had begun to exchange confidences as to which of them would be bridesmaids, and at what church the ceremony would take place. When they had almost come to an open rupture over the rival merits of veils or no veils, white lilacs or Jacqueminot roses for the bridesmaids, one of them ventured to rally Miss North upon the subject of her approaching nuptials, and was met by a sudden sharpness of rebuke she little counted on. Older gossips said what a very clever thing Mrs. Thornton had done to secure that fortune for her sister, as everybody must see Amy had been from the first quite thrown at Mr. Erskine's head.

To Erskine, whose whole heart and mind were filled with his consuming passion for Rosalie Gray, these reports seemed trifles light as air. His conscience acquitted him of anything more than the frankest brotherly affection for Amy; and he laughed when he sometimes told her of the charge. So absorbed was he in his own troublesome state of mind, that he never noticed a certain almost wistful gentleness that stole over the young girl when she talked with him.

Poor Erskine! He was in sore need of somebody's love, when the one he sought proved so elusive. He felt like an automaton, going through day after day of meeting and greeting Rosalie, only to go away cursing his folly in dreaming he could ever wake this Galatea to a response. It was madness to waste so many months of life and energy in haunting the footsteps of a strange adorable woman, whose winning tact and grace kept him within the bounds of civil commonplace, when an unguarded word or look of sympathy from her would have let loose the flood-gates of his tenderness. And yet—and yet—at times, since his return, he dared to fancy she was kinder to him than before.

It was within two days of the time fixed for his departure that Erskine, clad in his mountain costume, looking, as Amy North told him, with his rich coloring and sweeping dark mustache under the bold curve of his wide-awake hat, like Fra Diavolo about to sing a solo, appeared at the door of Mrs. Gray's cottage.

"You have always promised to climb the mountain with me some day. As I go the day after tomorrow, perhaps you will be good enough to give me this afternoon. Please do," he added, pleadingly, as she seemed to hesitate. "It will be the very last time. The summer is over now, and it will be all changed if we meet again in town."

Rosalie let fall her embroidery, and went off to prepare for the walk. When she came down again, she wore the dark blue dress with the crimson touches here and there, and the kilted petticoat, so well remembered by him since the day of their first meeting in the cave. They walked side by side across the yellowing fields, aglow with feathery plumes of golden-rod, and his eye rested on her with delight.

"There will never be any dress like that, to me," he said; "only there is one thing lacking—your bunch of daisies at the waist, and another in your hat."

"The daisies are all gone now, so I must take a substitute," she answered, lightly, stooping to pick some sprays of golden-rod. "How will this do?"

"Royally!" he said, with a sudden burst of his old boyish enthusiasm, so long under control. "No flowers that you have worn have ever seemed to suit you half so well! I can't picture you without flowers, but I think when I wake up in paradise, I shall like to see you standing there, decked as you are now, in these tossing golden plumes—"

"Please leave me out of your pagan arrangements," she said, laughing, and coloring deeply. "I am more inclined to come to the painful conclusion that Nature is giving me a hint to leave the daisies and betake myself to her autumnal garlands."

She made haste to divert the dangerous current of their talk into another channel. They passed through thickets where the sumac flamed, tall grasses bent beneath their weight of fruitage, and giant brakes spread out their layers of green. In the hollows, where in early summer hundreds of wild roses opened their pale pink petals to the wind, the forsaken plants now interlaced their briery arms, and clothed themselves with scarlet leaves and capsules.

There was a wild autumnal flavor in the air. The blue of heaven was overcast, the wind with a "saintly Memnonian swell" swept through the forest aisles. Far out, on the wide Atlantic,

> "Through scudding drifts the rainy Hyades
> Vext the dim sea."

The autumn gale was rushing shoreward fast.

"Are you afraid to go on?" Erskine asked, as they struck the mountain trail and set their feet upon its rocky spine. "I don't think the storm will be upon us before night."

"Afraid! never!" she answered, the spirit of adventure shining in her eyes. "I could walk forever in such an atmosphere as this. Besides, I have always longed to view the coming of a gale from one of these mountain-tops."

After a long and toilsome climb the summit was attained, and they stood there with the wind hurtling around them, wild and free. A wide panorama of sea and shore, hill and vale, lay at their feet. The outline of distant hills upon the main-land was dim and gray; the water all about the fairy islands was ruffling angrily; the storm-cloud from the ocean came ever swiftly on.

Rosalie stood upon a crag, with the garments blown back from her beautiful form.

"How glorious it is!" she cried. "I have never

seen it like this before. Fancy old Spouting Horn and Thunder Cave to-morrow, when the great waves go raging madly in, to break and scatter in a thousand flakes of foam!"

"The rain is nearer than I thought," answered Erskine, who had been surveying the clouds with some anxiety. "And although I feel a natural hesitation in requesting a storm-inspired goddess to step down from her pinnacle, perhaps you will remember that we have no umbrellas, and that the hour is later than that we calculated on to begin our descent."

She gave him a bright smile, and no longer, as in the ascent, disdaining the help of his hand, began springing downward from rock to rock.

"I suppose it is part of the initiation of the true devotee to Mount Desert to be lost or drenched at least once during the summer," she said, gayly. "What if both befall us now?"

Which did, indeed, seem impending. Erskine, who thought that he recalled a cottage situated upon one of the mountain spurs, had taken a path leading in that direction rather than risk the long unsheltered road to the village in the face of such a storm.

The trail they had been following stopped abruptly at the summit of a cliff springing from a grassy plateau at least twelve feet beneath them. The face of the rock was unbroken by crevice or projection; to descend it by ordinary means seemed a thing impossible. Half way up, the green branches of a fallen tree arrested in its crash by the rocky wall, spread out, concealing the trunk with masses of luxuriant verdure.

"I know where I am now, if that be any consolation," Erskine said, after a rapid reconnoissance of the situation. "I spent an hour down in that bed of ferns this summer surveying the cliff from below. The path leading from there is a cow-track to the very cottage I am in search of. But there is no time to waste, so here goes!" And in a moment he had swung down the cliff, supporting himself as best he could, and crashing into the branches of the fallen tree. Directly after, Rosalie saw his head and shoulders emerge from a mist of green leaves before her.

"Only care kills cats!" he said, merrily. "I am quite steady now, with my back against the rock, and my feet firmly braced on a stout branch of this friendly old tree. There is nothing for it but to let yourself down, and I will catch you. Don't fear, Mrs. Gray; it is really not dangerous."

Rosalie's answer was instant obedience. She let herself drop into the cloud of green, and was met by Erskine's arm, which closed around her in an iron grasp. The branches snapped and quivered under the shock of her fall, but the old tree bore up nobly, until, with considerable difficulty, they made their way down its sloping trunk to the ground beneath.

"That was an exploit!" said Rosalie, looking up at the level where she had recently stood. "I could not have believed it of myself; and as I let go and came crashing down upon you, I thought it was the most abominably selfish thing I ever did in my life."

"I won't tell you what I thought of it—yet!" Erskine answered, with a smile. "You have a great scratch on your forehead, your sleeve is nearly torn off, and the pretty mountain dress is quite defaced. Here come the rain-drops, and we must make haste to find a shelter."

They ran together down the steep path, parting the overhanging boughs, and reckless of where their feet were set. The rain fell in great pelting drops like hail, as they fled hand in hand. Erskine's strong clasp and his firm stride were an immense help to Rosalie when springing over mossy rock and fern thickets, and she found herself involuntarily quoting the fairy's answer to Puck, "Thorough bush, thorough brier," as they stopped for a moment to draw breath.

"'Thorough flood, thorough fire,' add for me," he said, "and to the world's end, joyfully, if I had your hand in mine. There is the cottage at last! One more scamper through this bit of wood, and we shall be safe."

It is such a common event in that region to give shelter to storm-beaten wanderers that the good people within the little house made their arrival quite a matter of course.

"You did get a pritty consid'able peltin', now, didn't you?" said the old woman, who escorted Mrs.

Gray into a rear room, resplendent with patchwork quilt and giant feather-bed. A little fire was quickly made, and an extraordinary flowered bed-gown produced in lieu of Rosalie's saturated garments. The old woman bustled in and out with cups of "yarb" tea and fresh sticks for the fire. Upon Mrs. Gray's inquiry for the gentleman who had accompanied her, what was her surprise to learn from her hostess that he was already some distance on his way back to the village.

"Here's a bit of a note he writ on a piece of the almynac; maybe that 'll tell you what he cal'lates to do."

"I am off to tell your aunt, and to fetch your dry things, and some sort of a trap to take you home. It is impossible for you to face this rain again."

Rosalie suppressed a strong feeling that she had rather far have gone with him, even through the driving storm. To get away from her thoughts she came out in her comical disguise into the little room, where two old men were sitting, one of them, evidently her host, a shrewd weather-beaten specimen of humanity, who had, like many of the islanders, a regular sea-flavor pervading him like a bit of old tarred rope. He was full of kindly gossip, and the absence of marked provincialisms in his speech arose from the fact that, until a few years before, he had followed the sea, and knew almost every port on the two continents.

"And your wife," said Rosalie, after hearing a

long yarn; "what did she do here during all your voyages?"

"My wife! Bless you, miss, you mean the old ooman there? She's my sister. I stayed by a gal once, but she died, and sence then I han't had any speret. I means as well by the gals as any man on the island, but I ain't mannerly somehow."

"Your sister makes you very comfortable here, at any rate," Rosalie said, looking round upon the hair-cloth sofa, the shells, the kerosene lamp, and the irrepressible tidies that banish from our humble homes in America every vestige of the picturesque.

"Well, I kinder rub along, with this and that. If I get as much as three hundred dollars a year to keep up on, I'm rich. There was a Congregation'l preacher here last year from down to Boston, and says he to me, 'I've got a selery of five thousand dollars, and it's as much as I can do on that to make both ends meet.' 'Five thousand dollars a year!' says I; 'why, you'd oughter have a gardeen!'"

The remembrance of this scathing scarcasm kept her host chuckling for some time after, and at intervals he was heard to murmur, "Five thousand dollars a year, and can't make both ends meet!" in tones of heart-felt wonderment.

"This is your brother, perhaps?" Rosalie hazarded, indicating the bent and patient old fellow who sat in a far corner.

"Dear me, no, ma'am; that's only Jabez Stubblefield. He's a new-comer on this island. We don't know nothin' 'bout his folks. When Jabez was a little chap, I've heerd my father say, the cap'n of a schooner brought him along this way. There was an East Eden man tuk a fancy to have the boy do chores around the house, and he applied to the cap'n to have Jabez stay. Cap'n he didn't exactly like to give Jabez up without a kinder little *swap*, and the upshot of it was the cap'n he took along a fine bull-calf, and the man he kep' Jabez."

"But that must have been — dear me! — ages ago," said Rosalie.

"Yes, Jabez he's a pretty old man, I guess, and he married here, and his old ooman died, and all his children. They're buried on the island."

"And you still call him a new-comer!" said Rosalie. "This conservatism is equal to anything in the Faubourg St. Germain."

"Well, I guess Jabez 'll stay here till he dies," the woman said, as she came in with some food, which she proceeded, not unkindly, to administer to the poor old patriarch, a "stranger in a land that knew him not." "There ain't nobody left now but my brother and me, and we've got enough for three. If my boys had lived, miss," she added, presently, coming to sit down by Rosalie, and speaking in a matter-of-fact tone, without a tear in her pale blue eyes, "ther'd 'a been somethin' to save for; but they're all dead. I had four of 'em, and they were all lost at sea except the one that died of the fever in port, down in South America.

I've got a picture of his grave, miss, and the letter the hospital folks down there writ me, under glass, if you'll please to look at it. My husband was a sailor too, but he fell out o' the riggin' in a gale, and was lost over here in Penobscot Bay when we weren't six years married."

The rain beat upon the roof, and Rosalie fell a-musing. Life seemed to her such a little thing, and love how mighty! Oh, if she dared — if she but dared!

There was a sound of wheels, a shout, and Rosalie, expecting the arrival of her uncle, ran to the door in her comical attire. It was no sedate elderly gentleman who sprang from the covered vehicle drawn by two stout mountain horses, but Erskine, who, with his arms full of wraps, bounded along the little garden path.

"Here are some things your aunt gave me. Of course she was for having Mr. Carson come; but, actuated by purely benevolent motives, I would not hear of risking his rheumatism in this storm. Then your maid was proposed; but the vision of that fine fly-away French creature appalled me, and I would have none of her. Pray make yourself comfortable now, and come, for the gale is growing steadily worse, and the wind is blowing great guns."

Rosalie assumed her own attire and, taking leave of her kind hosts, went out once more, with a strange thrill of pleasure, to face the buffeting of wind and weather. Safely consigned to the interior of the vehicle, she was so entombed in oilcloth curtains that she could only feel, not see, the vicinity of her friend, who sat out beside the driver, urging the sure-footed horses to their full speed along the road.

"Tell me," said her voice out of the darkness, and Erskine leaned back to hear, "about yourself. You must be thoroughly wet again. How did you change your clothes so quickly? Are you sure it will have no bad effect?"

"I prevented such a contingency arising by not changing them at all, but took some brandy, and put on my ulster instead. Don't give me a thought, please, that is not of congratulation. I am the most selfish mortal alive, if you did but know it."

"Home at last!" he added, as they drew rein before her cottage door. There was no time for more, for there were lights, and open doors, and welcoming voices, and a general uproar of rejoicing over the wanderer returned.

"To-morrow," whispered Erskine, in tremulous accents, as he lifted her to the ground.

XI

WHEN Mrs. Gray was at last able to dismiss her useful but too emotional Désirée, whose idea of rising to an emergency was to wring her hands effusively, to repeat "Mon Dieu!" a great many times, and to proffer a tisane of *eau de fleur d'oranger*, she retired to rest, but not to sleep, under the shelving roof of her cottage bedroom. The gale raged with increasing violence; rain fell in floods, and great bursts of wind bore incessantly upon the house front like breakers on a cliff. The walls of her little summer dwelling shivered with each repeated shock, and the bed vibrated sensibly. Sleep under ordinary circumstances would have been impossible, but to-night Rosalie was in a strangely nervous state. Memory was at her pitiless work, conjuring up a thousand phantoms that she would fain have buried forever. A most unhappy past rose before her, warning her against vain indulgence in human faith and love. "You loved once," it said; "with what result? You trusted once; did it bring you peace? Remember the hours when in anguish you prayed God to release you from a bond that was worse than death. And more than all," chimed in her better self, "remember your tacit pledge to a guileless girl, whose fresh young love may confer the happiness yours never could again!"

Rosalie's pride came to her rescue after a burst of bitter tears. "It is an infatuation," she said to herself, almost angrily. "A woman of my age, to whom vows of love are an oft-told tale, whose life is filled with the incense of perpetual flattery! Who would imagine—he least of all—that for months, ever since our first meeting, I have remembered him, and retained every trifle that recalled him, with folly worthy of a dreaming school-girl! His roses, that I traced to him, and still consented to receive. Shall he ever know that when I met him at last face to face, and passed him without speaking, it was because I had resolved to crush a weakness that made my cheeks burn when I thought of it? Since I have known him here, during this lovely summer-time—and to-day especially—there has been more excuse for me."

When a wild wet morning dawned after the long tempestuous night, Rosalie fell into the deep sleep of physical exhaustion.

It was verging towards mid-day when Désirée stood by her bedside with her dressing things and chocolate.

"Madame Carson desired a thousand tendernesses; and there is a monsieur—Meester Erskine—below, inquiring for madame's health."

With a fevered hand Rosalie wrote and sent to him these few words:

"I am ill with fatigue and loss of rest. If you go to-morrow, come here this evening, and I will try to see you."

The lapse of hours gave her resolution. She spent the day in her room alone, while the fury of the storm spent itself upon the island, giving place to a heavy rain blotting out all the life and beauty from the view.

At the Rodick the people who were left shivered through windy corridors, wrapped in shawls and ulsters, or huddled round a snapping fire of birch logs in the great barn-like parlor, declaring that they had been sea-sick all night from the rocking of their beds in the gale, and would leave in the earliest boat.

To Erskine the day was interminable. The Thorntons tried to woo him into their little sitting-room; but he proved a sorry comrade, abandoned even by the boys (whose delight in ordinary times he was), who with the instinctive selfishness of childhood shunned his moody countenance, as rats desert a falling house.

Grace was perplexed and anxious. The Counsellor, after reading his rather elderly copy of a New York newspaper till he had exhausted the advertisements, wandered over to the dancing-room at the Rodick, where Amy, with several other storm-stayed young persons, was organizing a set of glees around the piano.

From her post as leader Amy saw through the window her friend Erskine stalking up and down the long veranda in solitude. She made a motion as if to beckon him, but, on second thoughts, refrained.

When people met at the early dinner hour, Erskine was absent. He was striding through rain and mire along the road leading to Schooner Head, where he stood upon the cliff looking out at the cold gray wind-swept sea, and listened to the mad dash of the breakers, not yet rested from their wild night's work. When evening came at last, "the spirit in his feet" led Erskine with bounding steps to Rosalie's home.

Mrs. Gray's delight was to have a tiny sweet-smelling wood fire upon the old brass andirons of her hearth. To-night it sparkled cheerily, and the student-lamp burned soft beneath its crimson shade. Beside a table holding her pet bits of porcelain, her vanilla-grass basket with its tangle of bright-colored silks, and a vase of Venice glass with meadow grass and orchids, Rosalie sat, her face somewhat withdrawn from the light, that, dancing over her black drapery, brought out here and there the gleam of jet.

Nearer to the fire, swathed in the soft folds of a pale blue Chuddar shawl, dear old Mrs. Carson was putting the finishing touches upon a high-art sunflower, worked on a strip of kitchen crash.

Such a sweet peaceful scene it was, coming in from the darkness and the penetrating sea-damp without! Erskine's wild fancy, overleaping the minor details of a luxurious taste, saw only the fireside, and Rosalie waiting there—waiting for him! He pictured himself the proprietor of a fishing-lodge somewhere, and this the angel of his hearth. Poor fellow! He was quite out of date with his romances.

They talked a while, and presently in bustled Mr. Carson, who was a musical maniac, and carried off his wife to listen to the singing of a girl with a lovely contralto voice in the adjoining hotel.

Something in the irrepressible joy of Erskine's manner when they were left alone sent a pang to his companion's heart. A strange constraint fell upon her, and she became very pale. Suddenly she lifted her eyes to his, and spoke with great resolve.

"You are going away to-morrow, and I have asked you to come here this evening that I may tell you something. First, about yourself. You have never asked me for an explanation of my manner to you—my one unpardonable rudeness in the early days of our acquaintance, if we can even call it such."

"I never shall," said he, impetuously. "It is forgiven a thousand times over."

"That is like you," she said. "And it is because I know you as I do now, and want your friendship," she added, after a moment's hesitation, and in a lower tone, "that I must tell you about myself—the story of my life."

Involuntarily a wave of apprehension swept over him. This confidence boded him no good.

"You are comparatively so young—for you can't be more than a year or two older than I am—and so full of trustful belief in everything, that I hardly think you will credit me when I tell you that I am a woman without faith—restless, unsatisfied, impatient of everything commonplace; wont to touch the cup to my lips and dash away what I have scarcely tasted; fitful, arrogant, cased in an armor that is proof against all soft emotion, all lasting tenderness." How stubbornly she wronged herself! "Years ago I gave away my heart, and wrecked my happiness in a marriage lasting long enough to drag me through all the tortures of disillusionment. I loved with a girl's fervor; I suffered with a woman's capacity. The world knew nothing of my life, for to outward appearance I had all that a woman's ambition could ask. Beauty, power, wealth, a husband courted and popular; and I was, as I am, very proud. If we all wore our hearts in view under glass, like the people in the 'Palace of Truth,' how many of the prosperous of your acquaintance would be envied long, do you think? It is not fit that I should raise for you the curtain over my uncongenial domestic life. Such things are common enough, Heaven knows? I have been free now for some years, and I suppose—happy. Only you will see that I am not quite the woman you have thought me."

How bitterly she spoke! With what passion her low voice trembled! Erskine sat motionless. The light had gone out of everything, he thought; even the wood fire ceased to sparkle on the hearth. By-and-by she resumed, but in a far gentler tone:

"I have let you see enough of my real self, for it has given you pain. We shall part now, and you must try to forget the woman who has crossed your path. For me everything is finished; for you it has only begun. Strength, talent, high aims, will carry you onward. Let me hear from you again when you have won the love of some gentle girl, who will come to me and claim me as her friend. For all that you have done for me and been to me I thank you again and again. If I have learned to believe in friendship once more, it is you who have taught me."

"And you tell me to forget you!" he began, passionately, but was stopped by the pitiful sadness of her eyes.

The little French clock upon the mantel-shelf ticked with the beating of his heart. A burst of wind came wandering about the house like an aimless soul in pain. He looked at her for a moment without speaking, then took his leave.

The steamer *Lewiston* bore away next day a large gleaning from the crop of lingering visitors, among them the Thornton family, not quite so buoyant as when they came (who ever does leave a pleasant summer place quite cheerfully?), and Erskine.

As the boat ploughed her way past all the well-remembered haunts on "cliff and scar," he was standing alone by the railing, looking back. Amy North left her family and came to join him.

"May I speak to you?" she asked, with a girl's vivid blush suffusing neck and cheek and brow.

"Certainly," he said, rather wondering.

"It may be very rude of me to dare, but I can't help it. I will never speak of it again. I have never spoken of it to any one before." She seemed for a moment unable to go on for the faltering in her voice. "I don't think anybody has realized what you have been suffering this summer except myself. I know Frank does not, or Grace. But

I must tell you that I believe—oh! I am quite sure—*she cares, too.*"

And then, red as a June rose, and rather tearful, poor Amy fled away.

XII

AMONG the "distinguished departures" for Europe duly chronicled by the newspapers early in October was that of "Mrs. Gaspar Gray and maid." The gay world over after-dinner coffee, and on the club-house portico at the Jerome Park races, regretted that her house would be shut up during the coming season.

"A woman like that is an immense loss to society, by Jove!" Mr. Watson Webster said, confidentially, to a stranger whom he desired to impress with his own exclusiveness; "or, I should say, to a few of us whom she especially affected. She did not even show at Newport this year, but went off and buried herself among the aborigines somewhere. You see, the trouble is, my dear fellow, New York can't *hold* her stars. I'm thinking of a run over to make half a dozen country visits in England myself."

Grace Thornton was plunged anew into her vortex of philanthropic engagements. It was a great blow to her to find that Erskine and Amy, though still good friends, had no apparent intention of ever assuming any closer bond. Erskine was, during that winter, entirely given over to hard work. Society forgot him, and it was only at rare intervals that he dropped in upon the Thorntons to dine, romp with the boys, listen to Amy's ballads, and discuss with The Counsellor some knotty point of law.

And Amy, what of her? What of all such Amys in the world? They dress and dance, and beautify and cheer their homes as usual. When Lent set in, Amy became the zealous leader of a fashionable sewing circle for the poor, and her little class of Five Points ragged boys found her more than ever worthy of their adoring championship. When Amy laid hold of anything to do, she did it with her might.

Again it was summer-time. Sitting one day wearily working in his office there came to Erskine from Newport, in Amy's well-known dashing hand, a little note, like a waft of cooling wind.

"Did you know that Mrs. Gray has returned, and is on her way, if she has not already gone, to Bar Harbor? Grace and I find our life here at this headquarters of swelldom rather tame after Mount Desert.

"I rebel against eight-button gloves and lace parasols and basket-phaetons and morning calls; but Grace, who is at heart a snob, I tell her, likes it, and persuades herself that she is doing it all in order to be 'nearer to darling Frank.'"

It is one of the inalienable charms of that "Summer isle of Eden," lying off the coast of Maine, that in the height of the thronged season one can always find some forest solitude,

> "Where the gloom divine is all around,
> And underneath is the mossy ground—"

or a cave in the rocks, to sit gazing down into pools filled with starry anemones and all the multitudinous life of the sea, and be lulled into repose by harmonies of wind and wave.

At what, viewed in the wonderfully clear atmosphere, seems a stone's-throw from the main-land, a rock rises from Frenchman's Bay whose waves go courtesying up to powder it with spray. This proves, upon close inspection, to be a superb mass, riven asunder by a chasm, where at high tide the surf speeds in over beds of sea-weed, and, receding, leaves its tribute of a hundred starfish there. The tinting of the rocks, of red and blue and gold and purple, is blended with indescribable mellowness, and where the bare summits rise sea-gulls make their nests. Westward a bar of pebbly beach extends, where at low tide one may gather a boat-load of sea-wonders, coral, shells, and weed.

One afternoon a canoe shot across the water and headed for this point. Its occupant, a gentleman, sprang eagerly ashore, and lifted his frail craft upon the rocks above the line of the advancing tide. A few vigorous strides bore him to the summit of

Bald Rock, where a flag-staff of the Coast Survey indicates the finest point of view. His impatient gaze on every side at once was arrested by an apparition on the ground at his feet, which brought the warm blood rushing to his face. It was a woman's coarse straw hat, tied down with a loose scarf of crimson gauze; through the knot to one side was carelessly drawn a bunch of golden-rod.

Immediately he became aware of a presence other than his own upon this desolate spot. There, under an overhanging rock, looking southward, her head drooped somewhat listlessly, and one fair hand shading her eyes, sat the lady of his dreams.

She turned as, with the old joyous impulse, he called her name. In spite of her habitual self-control her face grew very pale.

"I have come in search of you," he said. "For an hour I have paddled about the bay, looking vainly, and at last fell upon the device of climbing up to these rocks to scan the horizon with my glass, hoping to catch a glimpse of a vagrant boat. The man over there at the boat-house told me that you were certainly seen pulling in this direction, and alone. But you must have flown up here on the wing of a sea-gull. What can you have done with your boat?"

"I left it on the bar," she said, with some surprise.

"Then the tide, which was rising when you landed, has carried it off."

Rosalie uttered an exclamation of dismay.

"How stupid of me to have let time go by like this. It was a longer pull than I thought, and I was tired. Oh! Mr. Erskine, if you will be good enough to look for my poor boat. See, a fog is creeping up. It is quite time I should be returning."

"Impossible to leave you!" he said, "The boat has drifted off, and somebody will find it, without doubt. As you say, a fog is coming in; and we are a considerable distance from the village. You must come into my canoe."

What inspired him, Rosalie asked herself, that his eyes shone with such delight and triumph.

"You are forgetting your hat," Erskine said, as they picked their way down the rocks.

"Oh, of course," Rosalie said, in some confusion, as in giving it to her he broke off a spray of golden-rod and placed it on his breast, after significantly touching it to his lips.

"If this be not the one you wore on the mountain in the storm last year, it is a duplicate."

"I am afraid I have an eccentric way of liking one pattern of hats for the sea-side, without regard for the laws of fashion."

"I should have known your hat among a thousand. I assure you that I felt like Robinson Crusoe discovering Friday's footsteps when I came upon it lying here where the sea-gulls perch, and knew it to be yours."

Both felt that a great many commonplace remarks were in order at that moment. In ordinary life a lady dropping quite unexpectedly from one part of the globe upon a "lone rock in the sea," with a man from another, is naturally expected to comment on the fact. Again and again Rosalie tried to speak, and could not. All of her proud confidence had failed her in her utmost need.

"At least you should tell me whence you came, and when," she said, when they were seated in the canoe, and gliding swiftly away from the ever-lessening pile of rocks.

"I came to day; I am here," said Erskine's happy voice. "Now if you want to know for what I came, that is easily answered too."

Rosalie was silenced, and the fog overtaking them just then, they were incontinently blotted out from the rest of the created world.

"Shall I tell you what I wish?" he said, as the delicious sense of utter isolation with her stole over him. "I wish that the fog would never lift, and that we might float on forever. It is like heaven to have you so near me, after all these months of cruel silence and separation. I have loved you, Rosalie, and followed you like a madman ever since my eyes first rested on you. There has never been a moment's wavering in my devotion. Fate has brought us together again and again, dearest. Why not hail it as a good omen, and stay with me always? Something tells me that I was a fool to have left you so, last year. Oh, Rosalie, do those blushes mean that I am right?"

"Oh no! no!" she cried, with as much energy as

one dare bestow on anything in a canoe. "Remember what I told you of myself. Don't make me suffer over again what I did then. After all, you are taking everything for granted."

"Tell me only one thing, Rosalie. Look me fairly in the eyes, and say that during all these months you have not carried in your memory what I said to you about the golden-rod. If you do not wear it now, because I love it—and *you*, my beauty—then, and then only, will I give you up."

What was there left for her but royal self-surrender? Erskine never so thoroughly realized the abiding inconvenience of a canoe as now.

The fog lifted, and before them earth and sea lay bathed in happy golden light. High towards heaven rose the blue outline of the everlasting hills.

UNDER THE CONVENT WALL

UNDER THE CONVENT WALL

About twelve o'clock one bright February day in Paris, Madame Bourget sat waiting for the arrival of her belated scholar, Miss Cora Bell, a young American whose habit it was to spend a couple of hours three times a week in so-called "elegant conversation" in the French language with that worthy dame. The little apartment where the teacher lived had formerly been a garret over the *dépendance* of a suburban boarding-house, taken under some stress of circumstances by its present occupant, and, little by little, with taste and perseverance, it had been made to "blossom like the rose." No wonder merry Miss Cora liked her tri-weekly French lessons. The walls of the large room, divided into two smaller ones by screens, were hung with fluted chintz, all flowers and leaves of brightest hue. A tiny porcelain stove diffused, when called upon (but that was not too often, for madame, like all Frenchwomen, believed in economy in wood), a friendly warmth. In the windows, whose panes of glass were polished like the speckless boards of the flooring, were kept plants and birds. A great green box of mignonette in flower sent out a luscious fragrance. Vines were made to start from behind every picture-frame and out of china jars upon the shelves; and somehow or other they grew like Jack's bean-stalk, strong and green and luxuriant. Best of all, a flood of genial sunshine came in on all sides, for the garret boasted of various windows. Where madame slept, one could find out by peeping behind a screen at the tiny white-curtained bed with the crucifix above it, but where madame cooked no one ever guessed; yet she had a fashion of producing from unknown corners a series of luncheons that were nectar and ambrosia to her youthful visitors. Days there had been in madame's past experience when the poor lady had known what it was to subsist upon the slenderest of rations, but now the fame of her exquisite embroideries in chenille and silk was noised abroad, while her occasional scholars, like Cora Bell and a few liberal Americans of the same set, made up an income sufficient for the widow's wants.

Madame Bourget, sitting at the open window overlooking an ivy-covered wall that just here formed the boundary of the Bois de Boulogne, felt quite wistful with regret over the non-appearance of her favorite scholar. "She will not come now," the widow said to herself, as the inevitable mantel clock struck a cheerful loud-voiced "one." "Truly, she has twined herself into my heart, that chère petite Cora. How she laughs and dances and sings her life away! Just like that other one—so many years ago." A shiver ran over the little woman's frame, and she closed her eyes as if to banish some painful image. "My pretty Cora will never know so sad a fate as hers, thank le bon Dieu." A light step upon the stairway, and Cora, blooming with health and animation, came into the room.

"Don't scold, dear madame. There is time enough yet for a chapter of our book before they send for me."

The lesson began, but Cora's attention wandered; her thoughts flew off at a tangent; her eyes grew dreamy; a deeper rose-color settled in her cheeks. At last a little white protesting hand was laid across madame's page.

"Bourget dear, I want to confess to somebody. Won't you be my priest? You know that papa is in America attending to business always, and that mamma is forever going out. I've nobody but that stupid Parker of mine, and talk I must — I must. Oh, Bourget, if such a thing can be, I am too happy! All of this dear blessed morning *he* has been with me, and mamma has given her consent, and we are to be married soon."

And then, the flood-gates loosed, came a stream of joyous confidence. Cora never thought to look up at her listener until she felt a hot tear, then another, drop upon her hands clasped in the widow's lap.

"What is it, dear madame?—what have I said

to pain you?" the girl asked, wondering, to be answered by a fit of bitter sobbing. With kind and gentle words Cora soothed her friend's emotion, and at last Madame Bourget was able to speak once more.

"Forgive me, dearest young lady," she exclaimed. "In truth I never can forgive myself. I owe it to you to explain my weakness. See here: this picture which you have often caught a glimpse of in my desk. Look at it — judge for yourself of her youth, her innocence, her beauty. She was my only child, and I have lost her forever. Years ago she knelt, as you do now, and poured out to me the wealth of her love and happiness, under circumstances like yours. The rest is too painful for you to hear."

"Tell me more," the girl said, tenderly. "I would be selfish indeed if I refused my sympathy at a time when all seems so bright before me."

Little by little the story was revealed. Ten years before, Léonie Blanchet had been sought in marriage by a wealthy Englishman, to whom her mother had given her with some misgiving, watching her go from that modest home into a life of luxury with many anxious fears. The husband Léonie had chosen was handsome, young, and winning; he had convinced her of his right to a rank and station far above Léonie's expectations. Léonie adored him. What, then, was there to apprehend? The widow could not tell — but still! Léonie's first letters came to her so full of buoyant pride, of confident happiness, that for a time the mother could not but reflect it. The young couple were absent upon their wedding journey in the South, and had reached Rome, when a thunder-bolt fell upon the pretty, trustful bride. It was a mock marriage. The man whom Léonie believed to be her husband had left his true wife in England—a gay, fashionable beauty, sufficiently "emancipated," according to the notions of her class, to scoff openly and lightly at her husband's latest fancy.

"But this is not for you to hear, my child," the little French teacher said. Cora, who from motives of delicacy had avoided looking at her friend, glanced hastily up, struck by the suppressed passion in her voice. What a transformation was there! In place of the quiet, repressed, demure personage she had been accustomed to see, Madame Bourget's eyes were afire; her cheeks glowed with a dull crimson; her teeth were clinched.

"Do you know what, had I been Léonie, I should have done to him?" she went on. "I am a Corsican, and the blood runs hot in our veins when it is stirred by wrong—*va!*"

The brief passion was spent. It was succeeded by a calm even more full of meaning. Cora waited until her friend could trust herself to speak.

"They parted then and there," Madame Bourget went on, in a low tone. "He did not defend himself. He simply laughed at her—my poor, heart-broken, humiliated child. He said she was too innocent for the times she lived in. And so she was, bon Dieu—too innocent. She put all of this into one last letter to me, and then she fled—fled into the night."

"And now?" the young girl said, after a long silence.

"Now she is at peace," the mother answered, quietly. "The Holy Church received her in its bosom. Léonie is one of the sisters of the convent of the Sepolte Vive. For some time past I have been laying up money in order to take the journey to Rome; but until recently it was all I could do to live here, and to go away from my employment meant starvation. Oh, if I could but have seen her I would have starved — yes, gladly —but that is impossible. All that is permitted to me is to visit the outside of the convent upon her 'day.' Once a year each sister has a 'day,' when she is allowed to throw over the convent wall a flower in token to her watching friends that she is still alive, but there it ends. I know what flower my Léonie would choose — a bunch of fresh white lilac!"

"'Sepolte vive'—buried alive!" the young girl repeated, sadly. A shadow seemed to fall over her life and her budding happiness.

A few months later saw the Roman spring unfold in all its glory. A party of tourists were visiting that relic of mediæval days, the convent of the Sepolte Vive. Most of them turned back disappointed at the threshold, but a group of three people lingered until the rest of the sight-seers, after a colloquy held beside a revolving barrel in the wall of the convent, had reluctantly dispersed. Over this barrel was traced an inscription: "Who would live content within these walls, let her leave at the threshold every earthly care." Upon these lines a woman dressed in black, standing apart from her two companions, kept her eyes fixed, while her lips moved in prayer.

The order of nuns who have thus condemned themselves to death in life subsists on charity. It is only when their supplies are totally exhausted that they are allowed, after twenty-four hours' starvation, to ring a certain bell, which the outside world interprets, "We are famishing." Two Lents are observed by them during the year — the one common to all Catholic Christians, and another held between November and Christmas. In the intervals the sisters receive and partake of whatever food may be bestowed on them by visitors.

Two of the three loiterers were young and handsome, radiant with happiness. That they were new-made husband and wife none could doubt, and it was a pleasant sight to see the wife order to be brought from a carriage in attendance a hamper of abundant dainties, and with the aid of her husband proceed to unpack their store. To attract attention from those within the convent the young man knocked briskly upon the barrel, which, slowly turning, revealed an opening to a shelf within.

"What wilt thou, stranger?" came a voice, faint

and far as the note of an Æolian harp. So strong was the sense of remoteness and of desolation produced by this sound that involuntarily the young wife clasped her husband's arm in shuddering.

"Oh! it is too sad," she whispered in his ear. "I think I shall go back to the carriage and leave Madame Bourget with you—may I not?"

"Nonsense, darling. Who is it who has contrived and carried out this little expedition, I should like to know? Come, cheer up, and bestow your bounties upon the good sisters within. Depend upon it they will relish them."

Their presents were given, and in exchange our visitors had received a series of *cartolini*, or tiny slips of printed paper folded like homœopathic powder papers, and intended to be swallowed whole by the believer, who might thereafter hope for a cure of any mortal ailment possessing him. As their colloquy with the unseen sister came to a close, the young man signed to Madame Bourget to draw near. The mother had kept a veil over her face while standing by in silence, but now she sprang forward, and uttered with feverish anxiety a few sentences of wild pleading unheard by her companions.

Fainter and farther were the pitying accents that smote her ear in return.

"'Sepolte vive,' daughter. The grave gives back no answer."

"Let us wait beneath the garden wall, dear friend," Cora said, as between them her husband

and she supported the steps of the trembling mother from the spot. "It should be at about this time that the flower is thrown, and oh! how it will comfort you to have it from her hand!"

Underneath the ancient wall of the convent garden the little group waited in silence. It was a moment of feeling too profound for words. As the hour drew near the mother left her friends and went to kneel alone upon a grassy mound where her cheek might graze the wall, as if caressing it. For a time all was silent. Then a bell sounded the hour with slow and solemn strokes. A bird burst into joyous carolling in the tree above where Cora stood. "It is a good omen," she said, glancing up into her husband's face. As the last stroke of the bell died upon the air something white and fragrant fell at the feet of the kneeling figure. "It is Léonie's white lilac!" Cora cried, starting joyously forward.

But the mother did not stir. The token had come too late to awaken joy or sorrow.

CHERRYCOTE

CHERRYCOTE

"And you expect me to travel over nine miles of muddy roads behind that beast and in that rattle-trap?" a gentleman said, discontentedly surveying the conveyance provided for him by an obliging countryman residing near the station of the Virginia railway, where a train had recently deposited the stranger.

"Well, 'tain't as ef thar was much to choose from, mister," was the answer. "If you've a mind to wait till evenin', the stage mout happen along. But, bless yore soul, sah, ole Buck 'll carry you thar ef you only give him time enough. An' I reckon the buggy won't break down 'tween this and the blacksmith's at the cross-roads. Thar's string an' rope an' a lot o' nails under the buffler-robe; an' little Poss here'll manage to mend the damage ef so it be that thar's a rock to pick up 'long the roadside."

"May I drive, boss?" was the hesitating prayer of little Poss (short for 'possum), as the dilapidated vehicle, drawn by a spavined plough horse, got finally under way. Looking down with amusement at his excited petitioner, Barksdale saw a droll little darky, costumed in meal bags, hatless, and with plaited twigs of wool, who, when the rope reins were relinquished into his hands, assumed the post of charioteer with dignity ineffable.

Barksdale forgot Poss as the overmastering power of early association soon took possession of him. Ten years before, at the outset of the war between the States, he had left the neighborhood through which they were now passing, and during that time the history of its places and its people had been almost a sealed book to the wanderer in many lands. He had fancied himself weaned from his sentimental love for old Virginia; but here he was craning his neck to look at the ancient landmarks, recalling rides ending at this point and picnics at another, his cheek flushing and a lump coming into his throat like the veriest school-boy home for the holidays. The country was beautifully green, and as old Buck plodded along there was nothing to do but to resign himself to memory and anticipation, while the wind, laden with fragrance from the blossoming woods, blew over him refreshingly.

At last Cherrycote Farm was reached; but before they could enter it, little Poss jumped down to struggle with an old red gate of such persistent inhospitality that Barksdale himself could only force it open by half lifting the crumbling gate-post from the soil.

"Barren acres," he said, with a sigh, glancing over what were once prosperous fields of grain.

Grass grew on the roadway, and a multitude of little blue star flowers were crushed beneath their wheels. Emerging from a bit of pine woods, he caught sight of the gables of the old house. They at least were unchanged, half veiled from sight by Virginia-creeper and wistaria, jasmine and roses. His old room was that one with the window over which grew the branch of a mulberry-tree, its foliage so thick that neither blind nor curtain was required. As Barksdale gazed he saw, emerging from the shrubbery around a turn in the road, a cavalier bestriding a sleek mule. This was a man seemingly between thirty and forty years old, his once clear-cut features overgrown with flesh, and wearing a brown beard that swept his waist. His frame, albeit a trifle unwieldy, was muscular, his eyes were of an honest blue; his seat in the saddle, even though the mount was of the unenviable class, admirable. His clothing consisted of a pair of corduroy breeches tucked into spurred cavalry boots, and a nondescript shooting jacket faded by sun and rain, with a broad-brimmed hat of straw, showing marks of home manufacture. At the first sight of Barksdale his brows knit inquiringly; in a moment he charged down upon the antique buggy with military dash.

"Lance, old fellow!" he cried. "It isn't possible!"

"Hal!" exclaimed the other, simultaneously, in a tone that meant much. Immediately two hands met in fervent friendship. Since these hands had grasped each other last a river of blood had flowed between them. Bitter words had been spoken, hot discussions had raged, party strife had swelled resentful hearts; but now, when the half-brothers met again, neither thought of anything but the early ties of blood and affectionate companionship. Barksdale, thin, active, embalmed in an atmosphere of foreign travel, his clothes scrupulously well cut, his speech refined to nicety, appeared at least five years younger than the bluff, sunburned squire, who was, in reality, considerably his junior.

They were the sons of a Virginia gentleman, who, a widower with one small boy when he was hardly out of college, had consigned the little Lancelot to the care of his mother's relatives in the North. Marrying a second time in Virginia, Mr. Barksdale had settled down to a peaceful agricultural existence on the estate belonging to his bride, "one of the Carters of Cherrycote Farm," as that lady was styled.

Hither Lancelot had come to spend many happy hours of irresponsible holiday in the free and easy life of old-time Virginia. Here he had learned to feel a sincere affection for his kind step-mother and her boy Hal. But at the outset of the war his Northern training and sympathies in political faith set a terrible stumbling-block in the path of family pleasantness. Unwilling to contest the fervid torrent of secession talk, he at first kept silent. This led to suspicion, and finally to open warfare on the part of the generous people who had once extended their arms to him. His father had died, and the widow, an ardent Southerner, learned to look on him with constraint. Even Hal, merry, handsome Hal, who had adored the ground Lance trod upon, began to quarrel with him. There was nothing for it but retreat. Lancelot returned to his Northern home, and soon heard the news that Hal had become a volunteer at Manassas. After that there was a long and painful gap in their relations.

It was while wandering aimlessly around Europe ten years later that Lancelot made up his mind to return to America, and to visit the home of his fathers. The resolution once taken was acted upon with almost feverish zeal. Now that he had again shaken Hal's hand, had satisfied himself that the slim lad of nineteen was still somewhere lurking behind the veil of adipose matter enshrouding the man of twenty-nine, Barksdale breathed a long sigh of relief. As for the squire, he was one of those guileless natures content to take things as they find them. Barksdale's foreign airs excited in him wonder not unmixed with amusement. He fell to speculating over what the women would say to this importation of fastidious elegance into their impoverished household. In old times Cherrycote had never speculated; secure in homely plenty, it had simply flung wide open its doors and bidden the stranger in.

"Suppose we walk the rest of the way," Barksdale said, springing with alacrity from his mouse-trap of an equipage. "I have so much to say to you, Hal, I don't know where to begin."

"I don't walk much nowadays; but still—" said the squire, getting down in rather a ponderous fashion, and leading the mule, followed by Poss and his spavined steed, along a road carpeted with pine tags and bordered with wild honeysuckles.

"I haven't asked you about your wife," Lancelot said, when it appeared that the question could no longer in common courtesy be deferred.

"Kitty? Why, she's splendid," said the squire, heartily. "And if you'll believe me, Lance, I have six young ones, all girls. The old house is as full as ever, but you'll find things down at the heel, I reckon. The same story everywhere hereabout: no money, poor labor, no repairs; the women struggling with inefficient servants, worn-out furniture, worn-out clothes. But Kitty's temper don't wear out, thank God! You've not forgotten what a splendid girl she was, Lance?"

"I have not forgotten her in the least," his brother answered, in a tone of slight constraint.

"You must have been surprised to hear I married her. When you left I was far gone in the direction of Polly Rivers, of Rivers Hall, you remember. Polly played the devil with me; was engaged to another fellow all the while she wore my ring. I saw her last year at the Old Sweet; and, by George, Lance, she's as big round as a barrel, and has three chins. Kitty, now, is slight, and has kept her figure wonderfully. I didn't lose much time in courting her after Polly bounced me, did I? She was always the jolliest little thing, was Kitty."

Lancelot thought of the time when he had last seen Katherine Morris, one of the many cousins of a youthful cousin of Mrs. Barksdale, on a summer visit to Cherrycote. She was standing in the deep grass of the old orchard, under the cherry blossoms, in the spring of '61, a mere slip of a girl then, with large dark eyes, and a weight of dusky hair upon her small proud head. He remembered the gown she wore, a sort of full-bodied thin white stuff, with a sash of crimson, and the trick she had of interlacing her small brown Southern fingers while she talked.

"Never, never!" she had cried out, in an impetuous treble, the sound of which still echoed in his ears. "What I promised was not to an enemy of my country. I had rather *die* than marry you."

She had faced him bravely, two red spots flaming in her ordinarily clear pale cheeks, but there was a tremble in her voice, as if she would have been glad to cry instead of speaking defiance.

Thus they had parted; in the course of time Lancelot had heard of his brother's marriage with "our cousin, Katherine Morris;" he was to meet her as the mother of Hal's six girls! For a moment he felt like turning back upon the threshold of his visit, but while little vagabond Poss was in quest of refreshment for man and beast, the two walkers struck into a well-remembered path across the orchard leading to the house. The cherry trees were in bearing now, and under a green arcade of fruit-laden boughs was seen a merry group of ladies and children picking violets in the grass.

Lancelot caught one glimpse of his old sweetheart, recognizing her instantly. From the girl of seventeen she had expanded into a splendid beauty of twenty-seven, lithe and brown as ever, with a rich color in her cheeks, not in the least suggesting a matron oppressed by cares of maternity and housekeeping. Swarming about her were a number of affectionate small girls, and at a little distance stood Mrs. Barksdale the elder, looking thin and careworn, engaged in conversation with a lady whom he dimly recalled as another Miss Morris of the bygone days, then a coquettish personage with dimples, and wonderful plaits of hair worn in a crown around her head. The dimples were still evident, though the cheeks had faded, and the abundant braids were perceptibly thinner. Barksdale took in all these details, while struggling to control the immediate and powerful impression made on him by the first view of his brother's wife. The color had receded from his face, leaving him quite pale.

"What is the matter with you?" asked Hal, innocently. "No doubt our Virginia sun has been too much after such a confoundedly long walk. I say, Lance, if you'd care to, come into the dining-room and let me mix you a julep before you meet the ladies!"

"Capital idea!" Lancelot found himself answering, with a strong effort at indifference. He succeeded presently, and while Hal bustled around among the decanters, calling for ice and mint and strawberries, stood battling with the ghost of his younger self. The trial had been to the full as painful as he had expected. Often as it had presented itself to his imagination, the reality was not surpassed. Her face had shone upon him like a star from Alpine heights, across wintry seas, in desert reaches, at the opera, in his dreams, on the pages of his books, everywhere, anywhere, during ten long years of absolute non-intercourse. It was not until she had been Hal's wife for several years that he heard at all of this marriage, seeming to him so extraordinarily incongruous and unsuitable. He still could not reconcile it with her appearance, her manner, her pretensions, now that he had seen her once again in the splendor of maturer womanhood.

The jovial good-fellowship of the kindly squire offended him. He felt as if he could not bear to see husband and wife together, to hear Hal's lanky girls claim her as their mother. But Lancelot Barksdale had a noble nature and a strong will. Resolutely he trampled out the fire that had so suddenly been kindled up within him. Kate was no longer—it was long indeed since she had ceased to be—the sovereign of his dreams. This brief madness at an end, he would be able to take her by the hand like a loyal and honorable gentleman as he was. His reverie was brought to a prosaic ending by the appearance of Hal at his elbow, looking like an amiable young Bacchus, so ruddy were his cheeks, so broad his smile of pride over the beaded goblet he now presented to the traveller.

"Drink this, my dear boy," cried the Virginian, "and if in your travels you have come across a beverage to beat it, may I never compound another julep!"

Absurd as it seemed to a man of Lancelot's temperate habits to partake of stimulants at the meridian of an afternoon in spring, he tasted, nevertheless, of the amber liquid, wherein strawberries coquetted with sprigs of mint in a mass of finely splintered ice. "Your brew does you credit, Hal," he said, gayly. "And now to pay my respects to the ladies. You haven't told me what welcome to expect from my step-mother. I'm in her debt for a long list of bounties in my boyhood, and to have been separated from her all these years through the estrangement of that miserable war has been a real pain."

At this moment in came Mrs. Barksdale the elder to answer for herself. She had been told by the servants of the arrival of a guest, and, with the usual cordiality of her kind, hastened in to do the honors. "My dear Lance," she cried, after a momentary survey of extreme astonishment, "I'm glad to welcome you once more to Cherrycote."

"If you knew how much those words convey to me!" returned Barksdale, with real feeling, taking her thin old hands and kissing them. "I am alone in the world since my aunt died, a year ago, and the ties of early association seem more potent as we get on in life, I think. At any rate, I have fairly longed to make friends with you all again, and such a welcome as you and Hal have extended to me heals many a wound of time."

"And I am far too old to indulge in rancor," said the old lady, tears coming into her eyes. "Now that our fearful war is over, I can regret the violence of feeling with which we went into it. Oh, Lance! I am glad your poor dear father was spared seeing his State conquered. I think it would have killed him. But let by-gones be by-gones. We must agree not to talk about the war. It was kind of you to come so far to see us once again, and we will make you comfortable, though things are not as they were at Cherrycote. I am sure you are pleased to find Hal married and settled so happily. His little wife is such a manager I have given up the house-keeping entirely into her hands. And those sweet children! Dear me! here I am forgetting that Kitty wants you to come out to the garden, Hal, to consult about the best place to set out the Lima beans. Don't tell her Lance is here, for she has not the least idea who it is. The children said it was Mr. Lewis come to see their papa about the sheep. Such nice girls Hal has; and such a good mother that little flirting Kitty Morris has turned out to be! Lance, you must be taken to your room. But here comes Hal again with his wife. Though you never knew her intimately, I believe, Kitty knows you well by reputation."

At this point, when good Mrs. Barksdale paused for breath in her flow of cordial greeting, Lancelot felt his temples throb, and a sort of mist pass before his eyes. Through the opening door Hal hurried, followed by a lady, and in a single brief and blissful moment Lancelot became aware of the fact that Hal's Kitty was *not* his own "bride of old dreams," whose spell went with him still. In plain words, Mrs. Henry Barksdale the younger was none other than the cousin with the dimples—also a Katherine Morris, whose given name had long ago departed from Lancelot's recollection—had he ever been possessed of it, indeed? In the confusion of his ideas during the moments that followed this discovery he was absorbed with a longing to satisfy himself at once about his Kate—the Kate. "The only one worthy of that sweet old-fashioned name," he said, in his joyous heart; for lovers, as we know, glorify everything even the homely nomenclature of ancestral days.

She came in soon to answer for herself, the little girls, as before, twining around her waist and clinging to her skirts.

"I wonder, Kate dear, if you remember my oldest son, Lancelot?" said good Mrs. Barksdale, with an accent of pride in her presentation of the new-comer.

The evening sunlight slanted through a western window of the old oak-panelled dining-room. Lancelot stood with his back to it, his face in shadow, but the searching radiance brought out every expression of her changeful face more lovely than he remembered it.

"You have not done me the honor to supply the lady's last name," he said, a new fear assailing him as he took her hand in his.

"Still Kate Morris, though a greater belle than ever," cried hearty Hal. "It's just occurred to me, Lance, that you and Cousin Kate used to be famous friends till you quarelled about the war. Don't you think it's time to take back hasty words and begin again, you two?"

"I have nothing to take back," said Lancelot, and Kate's cheeks showed that she understood him.

"Come, come," said the kind old mistress of Cherrycote, "as I said, let by-gones be by-gones, children. I'm sure Kate is ready to start in again where the war interrupted her — now, aren't you, Kate?"

"Are you, Kate?" Lancelot found himself, later, murmuring where she alone could hear. And Kate did not say him nay?

THE SHATTERED VIOLIN

THE SHATTERED VIOLIN

One evening when the cream of a "first-night's" audience flowed into the Salle d'Athenée, in Paris, where the great Joachim was advertised to wield his magic bow, among the row of first violins in Pasdeloup's famous orchestra, grouped upon the stage, sat Gustave Thorez, a gentle old enthusiast, with a trim gray mustache, smartly buttoned up in a well-brushed black coat, and the inevitable bit of red ribbon in his button-hole.

As the concert progressed, and the listeners, crowding the pretty little theatre, broke into wild enthusiasm after the maestro's unapproachable rendering of some theme of Bach, Gustave, in common with the rest of the orchestra, took up the refrain with that applause the artist's soul loves best, coming with generous spontaneity from his brothers in the guild.

On his final withdrawal, after repeated calls to the front, Joachim, in threading his way between the crowded musicians, their instruments and racks, passed close enough to old Thorez to be arrested by the look of rare and dreamy delight upon his wrinkled face.

"Thank you, *mon ami*," the great artist said, kindly, laying his hand upon Gustave's violin. "May your instrument never do less noble service to art than it has rendered me to night!"

To Gustave his speech was like an *accolade*. Thenceforward the violin, always dear, would be sacred to him, owning but one rival in his reverential love. His comrades smiled when, the concert over, they saw the *vieux moustache*, shouldering his treasure, march jauntily away with a glow of color in his pallid face.

Nearing his lodging, in a quiet street beneath the shadow of the Panthéon, Gustave quickened his pace to an almost martial tread. Mounting the five flights of a stone staircase, he gayly hummed the verse of a popular song.

"She will have reached home by this, and the supper will be ready. My mouth waters for the thigh of that cold roast fowl I saw her put away. Supposing that I don't tell her at once about my grand event? That will keep to give zest to the salad and the cheese. It will cheer my pretty Gabrielle, for she has been a trifle *triste* of late Pretty, wilful little Gabrielle! I have sometimes feared that taking Mademoiselle Cheri's place in the Cendrillon has turned her little head. *Tiens!* but I can feel beforehand the rose-leaf touch of her lips when she shall stand on tiptoe to give her old father *deux gros bons baisers* upon the cheeks!"

Gustave had reached the last landing, and was fumbling at his door.

"Gabrielle!" he called aloud, on opening it.

No answer, and his face fell.

"She will have been detained to sup, no doubt, with our good neighbor Madame Bourget," he soliloquized, stumbling about in the dark to find his matches. "What! no table spread for the hungry *vieux papa!* Careless *petite* Gabrielle!"

No light, no tempting little feast, no kiss of welcome, no answering voice! Not then, or evermore!

People who cared to join in the mad struggle for life and limb leading to a rehearsal of the Philharmonic Society of New York, during that period before the society fell into its long and trancelike torpor, to be aroused by the bâton of the wizard Thomas, may have observed among the violins upon the platform at the Academy of Music a blurred and sketchy outline of the old Thorez who had appeared upon the occasion of Joachim's début at the Athenée. The warlike mustache flopped drearily; the eye had lost its power to gleam or soften; the red ribbon on the worn old coat drooped like the banner upon a forsaken citadel.

Gustave had traced Gabrielle to America, and had thither come in search of her; but in the city of New York—that great receiver of unlawful foreign merchandise—the clew was lost. Obtaining a place in the orchestra of a reputable society, he had fallen into the groove of a solitary and unfriended life. Among the few who noticed him at all Gustave passed for an honest but *toqué* old artist, whose harmless mania was the worship of his own violin.

One Friday afternoon of a bleak December day, at the close of the Philharmonic rehearsal, Gustave passed out of Fourteenth Street into Broadway, where, sauntering aimlessly down the sunny side of the block, he saw a lady descend from a carriage in front of a fashionable shop. He did not recognize the costly wrapping of seal-skin, half shrouding a slender form, or yet the air of languid luxury. But whose was that beautiful veiled face, that tress of escaping golden hair, if not his Gabrielle's? Gasping for breath, Gustave held his violin against his breast and waited. When she came out of the shop on her way to the carriage he intercepted her. Without a glance, she waved him impatiently aside.

"Gabrielle!" cried Thorez, with all his broken heart in that single word.

The girl started, looked him in the face, and caught her breath.

"You are mistaken, my good man, or mad. Do you want charity? or shall I have to ask the aid of a policeman to protect me to my carriage?"

"Gabrielle!" the old man said again, falling back as if he had been shot.

At this juncture an interposing policeman took Gustave in charge, and, without elaborate inquiry, consigned him, with his violin, to a night's lodging in the station-house.

From that night of despair dated the downfall of his self-respect. His habits, before decent, lapsed from bad to worse and worst. Losing his standing with musical societies of the higher rank, Gustave still did not find it hard to earn a livelihood. Upon the first occasion when he was engaged to play for dancing at a second-rate ball, Gustave fiddled like a madman through the night, then went home to shed tears upon his desecrated violin. After work in the orchestras of petty theatres came music halls, then lower drinking dens. When once the old musician came out of one of these haunts to slink homeward in the gray of morning, he fell upon the icy sidewalk, and in trying to save his violin received a severe concussion of the brain.

Getting up from his cot at Bellevue Hospital, after many days of prostration, something of Gustave's better nature came back to him. The nurses in his ward, finding the old fellow expert and biddable, made quite a pet of him; and eagerly pecking at the crumb of a kind word or a look of sympathy, Gustave, during his convalescence, began hopping about in the sunshine of human warmth like a reviving sparrow.

One day in March, when the winds were working havoc with flues and chimney draughts, the nurse of a woman's pavilion ward called old Gustave in to try his skill upon a refractory stovepipe in her department.

Close by where he was set to work a screen surrounded one of the beds, and a litter stationed there told too plainly that the "feet of the dead" were about to be carried out.

"Here, Thorez, lend a hand, will you?" said his friend the nurse, coming from behind the screen. "We're short of 'elp this morning, and I'm in a 'urry to get this poor creature out of the ward at once. I'm all hupset with the night she's given me, and I can truly say a more pitifuller case never fell hunder my hobservation at 'ome or 'ere. Since she took the bad turn yesterday she's done nothink but jabber French and call 'Papa! papa!' She ain't got a friend on hearth that hever I see, and she such a reg'lar beauty! Heart-disease it was, and shame and misery, that did the work. Hit's all ready now; you take the feet, will you?"

Gustave obeyed, and mechanically did the work assigned to him. As the men carried their covered burden out of the pavilion through the open yard a gust of wind, blowing suddenly across the river, lifted the sheet from the shrouded form.

Then Gustave saw again the face of Gabrielle!

When dismissed from the hospital, he wandered back to his old lodging, where for charity's sake the people gave him shelter for a night, until nearly morning he leaned in a stupor over the table, resting his cheek upon the violin.

Just before dawn he lifted the instrument and tried to play. It was a faint and tuneless echo of the theme from Bach which Joachim had rendered at the concert of the Athenée.

Gustave dropped his bow and, seizing a fire-iron from the hearth, struck with all his force upon the violin, setting free forever the sweet spirit it enshrined.

When, a few days after, the rushing river yielded up her dead, the body of Gustave Thorez was washed in upon the Fort Hamilton shore.

Upon a high shelf in the cupboard of his room, beside the wreck of an old French opera hat making a dusty and feeble assertion of remote respectability, some people of the house found the shattered remnant of the dead musician's violin in which a mouse was rearing up her brood.

A HOUSE BUILT UPON THE SAND

A HOUSE BUILT UPON THE SAND

A WEDDING-PARTY was about to issue from the wide-open portals of a brownstone house in upper Fifth Avenue. As usual, a little crowd of curious street loungers had gathered around the awning to see the hackneyed yet ever-interesting ceremony of rice-throwing, together with the reckless launching into space of high-heeled slippers.

Simultaneously the inner vestibule doors of the besieged mansion were thrown open. From an orchestra hidden by a screen of palms in the marble hall came the strains of an inspiring march. A swarm of white-robed maidens and attendant men filled the entrance-way, leaving a narrow passage, down which came a page, youthful and smirking, conscious of many buttons, having in tow a fussy Frenchwoman of uncertain age, who made great show of a large alligator-skin dressing-case elaborately mounted in silver. A cab drawn up first in the line of carriages before the door received these ornaments to society, but not before they had been plentifully greeted with curbstone wit, affecting to mistake them for the newly-married pair. Next came the father, a slender, middle-sized, care-worn man, between fifty and sixty in appearance, but, in fact, some ten years younger. After him, walking alone with superb independence, smiling, answering the farewells showered upon her, leisurely, giving her friends ample time to survey all the details of her dress of brown velvet and sable fur, came the bride. She bade good-bye to her family with composure, and laughed at the showers of rice falling around them as she and the young man following her descended the steps, to where her father was already waiting at the carriage door.

"There, that's over, thank goodness!" she said when seated by her husband, who occupied himself in drawing a rug about her knees. "Good-bye, papa; I hope you charged Marie about the dressing-case, not to let it go out of her hands for a minute. I put Aunt Hope's diamond star in there at the last moment. Who would have believed that the old lady was good for diamonds? I had made up my mind to nothing but a book-rack or a paltry little toilet set. I'm so thankful she settled on that old case of grandmamma's books as Grace's wedding present and not mine. I wish, papa, that mamma would see all my things are properly packed at once to-morrow, and put away till we come back. I can't bear to think of their being fingered by curious people. Yes, we will write from Washington or Richmond. There, we are off, I suppose. Good-bye! Good-bye! I trust, Dick, we mayn't be starved travelling in that horrid southern country. But think of Grace and her cheap little bridal trip to visit Ned's relations in that old fogy village in Connecticut! I should think she would have more self-respect than to let such a thing get abroad about her. Dick, I do hope you saw Marsden's face during the ceremony. I stole a glance at him, for I wouldn't have missed it. He looked so dreadfully cross and blue—ha! ha! ha! Just as he always looked when he was following me around and I danced or talked with other men."

As the carriage drove rapidly down the long avenue Ellinor settled back with an air of perfect contentment.

"We certainly ought to be satisfied," she said, in a business-like way. "The thing has been done in style! Papa has been preaching so about economy of late that I'd no idea he meant to give us such a send-off."

Richard started. He had, strangely enough for a bridegroom who had just succeeded in carrying off the belle of her "set" and season, lapsed into a meditation of a somewhat rueful character. He was very much in love with Ellinor, but the parting with his newly acquired father-in-law had not been as pecuniarily reassuring as he could have hoped. Nothing had been said of the future arrangements of the young couple beyond a vague "Hope we shall see you both back for a visit at New-Year, my boy." A check for $1000 had been duly presented (and as duly, we may be sure, chronicled by the reporters for the fashionable news columns) to the bride by her father, together with as fine a silver tea set as Tiffany could furnish, and an elaborate trousseau. (The wedding outfit of this republican belle had been modelled in Paris after that of a young foreign princess just then entering the bonds of matrimony with an English prince.) The flowers serving to deck the house for the ceremony would have paid the house rent of the young couple for a year. The collation, the music, the dresses, were as costly as is usual on such occasions in New York. The new Mrs. Eliot also left behind her in a special casket—Aunt Hope's star, as we know, was allotted to Marie's care—crescents, bars, drops, and pendants of diamonds, together with a dozen yards of lace fragile as a spider's web, but much more convertible into cash. In the "spare room" of the paternal mansion were heaps upon heaps of bric-à-brac, from Venetian glass to painted gauze fire-screens, the customary offerings to an expectant house-keeper. In the cab preceding our young couple was an expensive, ill-humored, but correct appendage in the shape of a French maid. What more could Mr. and Mrs. Richard Eliot ask of Fortune at the outset of their career? Richard, it may be parenthetically remarked, was in receipt of a modest but uncertain income from the junior partnership of a firm recently entering business on their own account.

Before the crowd around Mr. Talbot's doorway had time to disperse, to their surprise, the large front doors again swung back upon their massive hinges, and another bridal train appeared within. This time the bride was smaller, slighter, less assured. She clung to her father's arm, and her husband, a stalwart open-faced young fellow, shook hands right and left as he passed down the line. Instead of music from the orchestra, the cheery roar of a college song was started and taken up with good-will by the company. And just as the fair young bride turned for a moment to wave her acknowledgment from the threshold a small, elaborately dressed child ran out from the group, and clung, weeping, to her neck.

"Oh, Gracie, Gracie! what shall we do without you?"

The little girl was comforted and caressed, and Grace turned again to her husband; but her path was beset by servants and old family retainers, who kissed and showered blessings on their "sweet young lady." When, amid a rain of flowers and rice and slippers, the second bride had reached her carriage, she was observed to turn and throw herself impulsively upon her father's breast, whispering in his ear, manifestly to the surprise of his decorum and his shirt collar. What she said—this poor, unconventional little Grace — was, "Bless me, oh, my father!"—and the man of business, swallowing a decided lump in his throat, kissed her again, brushing the tears from his eyes as he muttered a few unwonted words of benediction above her sunny head.

No maid or lackey accompanied this couple, and their surroundings were so unobtrusive that the crowd upon the sidewalk gave vent to audible remonstrance at what in their judgment seemed an unequal distribution of parental favors.

An hour later all the guests had gone; waiters ran to and fro with piles of used plates, and solaced themselves at intervals with hidden bottles of champagne. The musicians were packing up their instruments in green-baize bags; the little male and female Talbots were skirmishing on the stairs, unwilling to succumb to bedtime and to nursery authority. A few remote relations, members of the family unearthed for weddings and funerals, were seen wandering around the house, peering into shut rooms, and handling with itching fingers the wedding presents, over which a Gorgon-like maid kept guard. An elderly cousin in black silk, festooned with an antique shawl of llama lace, was discovered—no one knows how she got there —in the butler's pantry ogling an untouched Strasburg pie, while a pocket-handkerchief full of grapes, cakes, and mottoes lay suspiciously near at hand. Another spinster made it her business to go around among the wax candles, snuffing them out with commendable economy. In the large drawing-room Mrs. Talbot herself, looking the picture of fatigue and woe in her trailing satin and Venetian lace, had dropped into a crimson satin chair, the two school-girl daughters on either side of her lost in happy dreams of future possibilities of their own. In a carved chair at the fireside corner, erect and placid, Aunt Hope, a shrewd-looking widow, sat at her knitting. Everywhere were drooping flowers, furniture pushed into unwonted corners, the general air of discomfort after the feast that entertainers know so well. Poor Mr. Talbot wandered about, getting in everybody's way, snubbed by the hired waiters, who failed to identify him as the proprietor, restless and dispirited.

"As it is now half-past seven, and there seems no reasonable prospect of dinner here, Maria," he said at last, after assisting the butler forcibly to eject an intoxicated hireling who was found sitting with his head in a punch-bowl amid a wreck of broken glass, "I think I'll go down to the club and get a chop and a bottle of claret."

"No, indeed, John; you must wait for us. There'll be something presently. Sit down here with Aunt Hope and me. The girls have gone to a 'rose-bud' dinner at the Mays', though I can't say I approved of it, before they are even 'out!' But they were so *set* I just gave them leave for the sake of peace. Heigho! our two oldest gone, there'll be these two to launch next winter, John, and a coming-out ball of course. How lucky that one can give such things at Delmonico's!"

"I wish you'd please to take another time than this, Maria, to talk about your Delmonico balls and fallals. Wait till these bills are paid, and see what they amount to. And what with George at college, and Tom at Dr. Blank's, and those two little chaps in the nursery, it's nothing but pay, pay, from morning to night."

"Well, John, I think you are very ungrateful, for a fine family like ours, to begrudge giving them all the young people they associate with expect," said Mrs. Talbot, tired and ungrammatical. "Just as our two poor girls are married and gone, too."

"Wait till John has had his dinner and he will sing a different song," said Aunt Hope, cheerily; and dinner being just then announced, John did brighten up as was predicted.

But not for long. Aunt Hope, who rarely left her country home to visit her city relatives, was struck with the jaded look her prosperous nephew's face had assumed of late years. His once active step has begun to lag, and an unwonted peevishness had taken the place of his light spirit of yore.

"And what will Ellinor do on her return?" Aunt Hope asked, when they were again talking over affairs. "What a queenly creature she was, to be sure, under her veil!"

"What does everybody do?" asked Mrs. Talbot, complacently. "They will probably not want to go to house-keeping at once, since Ellinor will be overrun with engagements, and I have advised Mr. Eliot to take rooms at the Hotel Guelph, where their meals are served, don't you know, and Ellinor will have no cares, no responsibilities. Of course we will furnish the rooms, and I am to go to-morrow to meet Palette. He has such taste, you know; and with all Ellinor's presents their rooms will be a *dream!* The only thing to really worry over is that poor Ellinor will keep no carriage at first. Mr. Eliot was quite positive about that, much to my surprise. Luckily I can call for her for visits, and they can have cabs for going out to dinner. I think it is the most delightful arrangement—this living at the Guelph. Just fancy! Ellinor will have absolutely nothing to do but to amuse herself."

"I had rather not think of it, Maria," Aunt Hope said, with unusual gravity, which was quite lost upon Mrs. Talbot.

"Of course, with Ellinor's looks, we had a right to expect everything in her marriage, dear girl; but she was absolutely infatuated with this young man, and, to be sure, he has always held the best place in society—invited everywhere—and dances to perfection. His ideas and tastes are just like Ellinor's, and he has been lavish in flowers during the engagement. He is never seen anywhere except with men from the —— and the —— clubs, which with Ellinor is everything. She is so fastidious. I only wish he were a little more independent in his circumstances; but of course John will arrange all that."

"Of course John will do nothing of the kind," said Mr. Talbot, with apparent effort. "We might as well understand each other, Maria, about this matter. You know whether I have held back any of the money I have worked so hard for all these years. You and the children have had it, every bit. I have written a letter for Ellinor, which her maid will give to her, telling her that I will continue the allowance she has had to dress upon heretofore. Anything more is literally impossible in the present state of my affairs, either for Gracie or herself."

"Gracie," said Mrs. Talbot, trying to conceal the blankness of her countenance. "That girl is a perfect enigma. Not content with saving at least two-thirds of the money her father gave them both for their trousseaux, and buying herself an outfit like a Quaker's, she has actually persuaded Edward that it is better for them to begin house-keeping at once. They have been off together (luckily it is in a quarter where nobody goes), and they have hunted up a two-story house with a box-garret—the most dingy, absurd little mouse-trap you ever saw—on the east side of the town, in —— Place. I believe it was occupied by a dress-maker last. The worst of it is, they have actually taken it, and have set the painters and paper-hangers to work there. Of course I did everything I could to talk Grace into an apartment. Everybody goes into apartments now, and you may be as poor as you please in one of them, and still keep up appearances. But Grace says that Edward is too big for any apartment she has yet seen, and far too noisy. And Edward says he wants four walls and a front door-step all to himself. He is as obstinate as a mule, it is plain to see, and I pity poor Grace when the honey-moon is over. What will become of her music—for she certainly has a lovely voice, and has had every advantage in masters—and her languages, and all, tucked away in that hole, with that kind of a set, selfish man for a companion? Just imagine what a house it must be when I tell you that they got it on a lease for eight hundred dollars a year!"

"I remember, Maria," said John Talbot, gently, "when we first came here from the country, and I was a clerk on a small salary, that *we* lived in one room of a boarding-house, and had to be content. Aunt Hope, I see you taking all this in in your quiet way, and I know it astonishes you. That a mother should reproach her child for trying to live within her husband's means, I confess, astonishes even me."

"Now, John, when you try to be satirical I always stop," said his wife, comfortably. "Haven't you, I'd like to know, always paid every bill without inquiring into it, and given the children every advantage without counting the cost?"

"Aye, God help me, so I have!" said John Talbot, getting up abruptly to leave the room. "Without counting the cost."

"John is like that sometimes," said his wife. "Don't mind him, Aunt Hope; he is really the most indulgent creature living. A true American father, some one called him, who met us at Nice last year. What puzzles me is this holding back about increasing Ellinor's allowance. Of course he must be talked into it. A girl of Ellinor's tastes, indeed! Ellinor *must* have money."

During a mild week in May, about six months

after the double wedding, Aunt Hope was again in town. She had called once or twice at the Hotel Guelph before gaining admission. The man in waiting at the entrance door took her card, glanced superciliously at her poke-bonnet, "guessed" that the madam was not receiving, and after a long delay came back with the information that Mrs. Eliot, at 2 P.M., had not yet left her room. At last Aunt Hope received permission to ascend to her niece's quarters, and being enclosed in an elevator, was carried to the sixth story of a sumptuous apartment-house. A boy in buttons answered her touch upon the electric knob, and conducted her through a long dark passage-way into Mrs. Eliot's presence.

Ellinor was lying on a couch in a small room littered with bric-à-brac, and crowded with furs, heavy draperies, and costly rugs. What light there was came through thin curtains of amber silk hung beneath screens of multicolored glass. A wood-fire was blazing on the hearth, and the air was perfumed to suffocation with the odor of roses and hyacinths, crowded in vases upon every shelf and bracket. A small stand of gilt wicker at Ellinor's side contained boxes of bonbons, fresh heliotrope massed in a yellow jar, the morning papers, and a couple of French novels. Amid this luxury the young wife lay in an attitude of utter listlessness, her robe of white India silk half hidden by a covering of gold-embroidered Oriental stuff thrown across her couch.

"Humph!" said Aunt Hope, sitting bolt-upright

on the edge of the first chair she could find. I supposed I had got by mistake into the room of some tragedy queen. What would your grandmother Talbot have said to this, I wonder?—she who was up by candlelight winter and summer, sweeping, dusting, cooking, mending, to make both ends meet, and to give your father and the others what education she could afford! Seems to me, child, the size of your rooms isn't in keeping with your finery. Of course, with a limited income, you *have* to live high up, that should be no reproach to you."

"I wonder if you know what we pay for this apartment," Ellinor said, sharply, naming a sum that made the old lady's spectacles fly off in her excitement.

That Aunt Hope had much to learn, she discovered in the course of this memorable visit. She found in her niece a type of an increasing class, descendants of the thrifty New York merchants of a generation back—cradled in luxury, and yielding to no hereditary nobles the right to surpass them in personal indulgence of lavish tastes. On every side in the circle of Ellinor's contemporaries might be seen the same push and struggle for supremacy in the world of fashion—a world of self-constituted aristocracy, whereof the puppets representing men and women danced to the far-away pipings of a social leadership they affected to despise, creating, in a word, a London at second-hand. In such hands the vigor of the American republic is swathed in eider-down and stifled in attar of rose. No wonder that a shrewd old woman like Aunt Hope, whose eyes had been wide open to the interests of her fellows these sixty years past, should pause aghast at the spectacle! A brief interview with her niece revealed far more than Ellinor meant to show. Already the husband and wife had begun to drift apart, both finding in the narrow limit of home companionship meagre food for their restless spirits. Night after night Ellinor went into the world, day after day lounged upon her sofa until the hour arrived for some fresh gayety. The discovery that, for the first time in her life, money to lavish on her own amusements was not forthcoming was resented as a personal affront put on her by father and husband both. On his side Eliot, a good-natured and well-meaning young fellow in the main, waked up with dismay to the reality of his married life. Instead of a helpmeet he had a princess on his hands. Little by little dreams of domestic happiness took wing. His pecuniary responsibilities overwhelmed him. In despair, he went back to the old society life for solace.

"Whose fault is this?" Aunt Hope asked herself, sternly, pinning her little gray shawl to go down the stairs, heart-sick and despondent of better things. Second thoughts induced her to turn her steps in the direction of the remote locality where Grace Fielding had made her home.

The small brick house in unfashionable ——

Place was blushing in a fresh coat of paint, and the brass dragon knocker on the dark green door shone resplendently. A tiny grass-plat was filled with tulips, hyacinths, and wall-flowers. From the open windows of the parlor Grace's voice was heard singing at her piano. A hand-maiden whose smile assumed personal interest in the caller ushered Aunt Hope into the presence of her niece. Grace greeted her aunt joyfully, and forthwith began the eager exhibition of a young wife's first belongings.

"No, dear auntie, you can't sit down until you have admired our skill in making sixteen feet square do the work of twenty. No crowding either; we *are* proud of that," she said, in her rapid, girlish way. "With the bookcases, which, thanks to your blessed wedding present and Ned's college library, we have filled, we defy criticism as to the decoration of our walls. Those engravings and photogravures and the little Florentine mirror look well, don't they, against the Pompeiian red, though 'tis only 'water wash?' The tops of the shelves, you see, have served to accommodate the best of our wedding 'loot,' as Ned calls it; but the china ornaments have by his stern decree gone into one especial press in the dining-room. We are rich in lamps and candelabra, of course, and the horrid little chandelier was banished altogether from this room. A committee of two or three of Ned's artist friends came here and 'sat' upon our affairs while we were furnishing, so we flatter ourselves that the tone of everything is eminently correct. That portière was an extravagance, but—don't tell—we exchanged a hideous rug for it that somebody bestowed on us. Now for the dining-room. Isn't it a pretty spot?"

Here, instead of the traditional gloom of the modern eating-room, were light, color, fragrance. Two little windows had been knocked out to be replaced by an ample bow, large enough, when required, to contain a tête-à-tête breakfast table. The furniture, of the slender-legged mahogany variety, glittered brilliantly in a bath of morning sunlight. Glass, brass, silver, and procelain caught up and repeated the sparkling effect. Two or three jars of blue Delft held vigorous young palms. A bowl of yellow tulips ornamented the centre of the table, and around the little plot of ground behind the house wistaria, ivy, and honeysuckle made a wall of green to enclose a grass-plat with its central flower bed.

"The wonder of it is, we are, in our modest way, a social success," Grace went on. "All my friends among the girls followed me here, and once a week I have afternoon tea, and so many pleasant people drop in. Now and again a carriage rolls into the street that brings all our neighbors to the window; but many of mamma's friends have contented themselves with sending cards through the post. The visits of mere form will soon stop, and then Ned and I will settle down to making our own "set," if we are to have such a thing. Think of papa coming, aunty!—papa, who never goes anywhere but to the office and the club. Sometimes he and the children have their Sunday dinner here, and we have great fun. Ned and papa are such friends! But then everybody is friends with Ned, Aunt Hope. We see less of mamma, because she is really very busy going out with Ellinor, and then she doesn't like to bring the horses to the east side of town."

They had luncheon, served by the smiling Phyllis upon flowery china, and afterwards Aunt Hope fell to sentimentalizing in Grace's æsthetic three-cornered chair by the open bow.

"There is nothing like the spring-tide of married life," the old woman mused. "How beautiful is this fulness of faith in the object beloved—this persistent happiness owning no alloy! Bless me, child, I am doting! Give me a cup of tea, and then you may—as I see you are dying to do—talk about Ned's virtues till one or the other of us drops through sheer fatigue, and I know which one of us that will *not* be."

Grace needed no further invitation. She sat down on a cushion at her aunt's knee; but before the confidence had gone far it was interrupted by a loud knock, followed by the appearance upon the scene of John Talbot, looking pale and worn.

"Papa," cried Grace, "you here at this hour! Has anything happened?"

"Don't be alarmed, my dear; we are all well at home, thank God," her father said, dropping wearily into a chair. "I am glad to find you here, Aunt Hope, you and Grace—brave women and true. I believe I am a little tired, that's all. The way has been long and hard, but my good name's safe. Yes: no man can say John Talbot has robbed him of a dollar. But for your poor mother and the children I'd not mind. There is a relief in all being known at last . . . Talbot & Co. have to-day failed to meet their obligations, and—I'd rather not talk of it just now with Maria and Ellinor and the rest."

By the time summer was fairly under way, the old farm-house where Aunt Hope had spent so many lonely years was alive with the clamor of young voices. Its long-closed doors had opened wide to receive John Talbot's family, of which the younger members made no scruple in declaring their delight at the exchange of domicile. Mrs. Talbot could not be brought to think of herself otherwise than as a much-injured woman. She wore away the long dull hours of country life in vain repinings for her lost estate, and her one gleam of light was the prospect of a visit with her daughter Ellinor to Newport later in the season. To read in the society journals of Ellinor's appearance in the Park or at the races, or of Ellinor's toilet at ball or dinner, was the solace of her present life. Grace and her husband spent their holidays at Hope Farm, and "the boys" rallied there from school and college. Mr. Talbot came but seldom, for a Sunday, when he could. He was back again at the treadmill round of business, and through the generous support of his friends had every prospect of renewed success. True, Aunt Hope, Grace, Edward, and the family doctor urged upon him rest; but the reproaches of his wife and the goading sense of responsibility to his children made Talbot shake his head and redouble his exertions. For a year this state of things went on, until one day in the following June, Talbot arrived at the farm with a look of rare excitement on his pallid face.

"I've got the reins in my hand again, Maria," he said to his wife, before the family. "Affairs are going on better than I dared to hope, and, please God, before long I can give you all I robbed you of."

"Father dear, how can you?" Grace cried, covering his trembling hand with kisses and with tears—"you, who have been so generous, so self-denying, so tender. Speak to him, mamma, and tell him this. He wants it from you, not me."

"Well, I'm sure everybody knows how well I have borne this trial—" Mrs. Talbot began, but was stopped by an alarmed gesture from Aunt Hope. Grace's arms were around her father, her cheek pressed to his. She did not see the strange look that came into his eyes as he reeled and fell heavily to the floor. By the time they could lift him to a couch it was found that life had fled.

As if through a mockery of fate, the following day brought Ellinor Eliot, alone and unattended, to the shelter of her aunt's despised home. Discarded by her husband, and overshadowed by the odium of a scandal with which the newspapers in another day would teem, she had come to her family for shelter.

"I shall always think that this misfortune of poor dear Ellinor's would never have come upon her," said Mrs. Talbot, the day after her husband had been laid to rest, "if John had taken my advice about allowing them enough to keep up the position she had always had. But there is enough left, I believe, for us to have a house in town next season; and she, poor girl, will be able to live down the consequences of her father's lack of judgment. One comfort is, she is still the most beautiful creature of her set."

For some years the little house in —— Place continued to be, in the eyes of two people at least, the centre of earthly sunshine. Wooed by the fame of its hospitality, guests came and came again, to go away singing the praises of their hosts. When, at last, to these young people fortune arrived in a measure enabling them to answer the demands of a growing family to widen the borders of their home, the change was made with infinite reluctance.

"One thing I can say with truth, Aunt Hope," Grace cried, impulsively, when the dear old lady appeared at the christening of a fourth young Fielding—"that the only tears Ned has brought to my eyes since we were married were shed when he drove me from our first home."

Aunt Hope smiled, but as she stooped to kiss the baby a tear fell on its face. She was thinking of John Talbot's wrecked happiness, of the mistaken struggle of his life.

ON A HILL-TOP

ON A HILL-TOP

One afternoon, in Central Park, when the late spring was making strenuous efforts to assert herself by means of shivering green fringes hung upon naked boughs, and by a tinge of red, like a blush for tardiness, over the bushes of *Pyrus japonica*, the main drive offered the usual spectacle of pleasure-seekers on wheels, rolling at a discreet rate of speed between Fifty-ninth Street and One Hundred and Tenth Street and back again, while keeping carefully in view each other's equipages, horses, grooms, and gowns. Not so brilliant in variety is this dress-parade of American fashion as that familiar to the lounger in Hyde Park or the Bois de Boulogne, but sufficiently gay and changeful to enchain the watcher's eye during the hour or two when its glory is at the height. Passing in review the rapid succession of coaches, landaus, victorias, broughams, wagonettes, T-carts, tilburys, and village-carts, sprinkled with less pretending buggies and hansom cabs, a young man on horseback kept his spirited steed in check, curveting back and forth where one of the equestrian roads crosses the principal drive, until a trig policeman began to cast upon him side glances of a decidedly investigating character. Evidently the loiterer's wait was in vain, for a look of annoyance came upon his open face, and giving his horse an unreasonable cut with the riding-stick, he at last consented to gallop away from the spot he had so long haunted. At that moment another steed, cantering lightly along the bridle-path, emerged from the trees ahead, bringing face to face with him a pretty girl with golden hair and a bunch of narcissus in the breast of her well-cut habit.

"You told me you were to drive with your mamma!" abruptly exclaimed the young gentleman; to which the lovely Amazon replied, blushing slightly and tossing her head, that she could not know she was obliged to render an exact account of her doings to every person with whom she might chance to dance at Mrs. Gardiner's ball. The groom coming up at this juncture diverted conversation from an apparently threatening channel. In the most natural manner our young man's horse was turned, and the couple were soon making their way through the suburb on the west side of the Park, to emerge upon the beautiful Riverside Drive. Here a wide and admirably made road runs parallel with the Hudson, whose tranquil bosom, skimmed by white-winged sail-boats or scarred by bustling steamers along the channel, reflects the wood-crowned summits of the Palisades opposite, and the colors of the sky.

"To enjoy the Riverside," the young man said, "one should resemble the 'true love' of the early English poet, who 'looks not back, his eyes are fixt afore.' Let me recommend you to impose a forfeit on yourself for turning your head one moment from the left as we follow up the avenue. In this way you may be able to preserve the illusion that you are out of town."

"It's all of a piece with everything else here," the girl answered, with a discontented glance at the landscape on her right. There, amid a curious combination of squalor and ambitious architecture, she saw on the steep slope in front of a squatter's shanty, in a wilderness of rubbish and tomato cans, two belligerent goats assuming the attitude of the supporters of the British coat of arms. Beyond an expanse of rocky hill-side, streets and boulevards were in various stages of construction. Here a brand-new feudal castle, looking as if it had come out of a bandbox, arose beside a whitewashed cottage with dilapidated roof and shutters. There a smart Queen Anne villa overtopped a road-side saloon for the sale of beer to wayfarers. Where a glimpse was caught of the elevated railway, the trains looked like caterpillars crawling along an immensely high and inexplicably long bridge. Gangs of workmen, steam-drills, piles of sand and granite, everywhere obstructed the neighboring streets. To see what still remained to be done might have depressed the most naturally sanguine spirit, save for the consoling evidence of what had been already done by the great city spurning her island boundaries in eager growth. To Miss Caroline Heath, aged twenty-one, recently returned from a six years' residence in Europe, the incompleteness of American affairs in general was a matter of continual comment. Edgar Barclay, on the contrary, the son of a Western man, who after making a fortune in Cleveland had moved to New York to spend it, was a warm defender of our peculiar institutions, and, coming from other lips than those of the present critic, would have resented unflattering comments upon them with emphasis.

"You are a most unreasonable person," he answered. "A few months ago you were raving about our 'atmosphere.' You declared yourself thankful to be a native metropolitan."

"Perhaps that was because I saw it was the only thing *you* could not boast of," she said, saucily. "I can imagine a Cleveland man feeling quite awe-stricken by New York antiquity. But for *me!* Have you forgotten that ever since I was twelve years old I've been roaming about Europe, absorbing by-gones, living in delicious old palaces where tragedies had taken place centuries before I came there? Why, I'm saturated with that kind of thing—tinged, like the bowl of a pipe. Think of Florence and Venice, will you, and contrast them with this. And then England! The last house mamma took there was a lovely old grange surrounded by a dry moat, and by trees and hedges, and turf so green and soft and unbroken that it made one adorably sleepy merely to stand at the window and look out."

"I should prefer to keep awake."

"Not if the only amusement you had was to walk down pretty green lanes, where the trees met overhead, to call upon the rector and his wife or the squire and his. When that was done, we waited till they came back to call on us. I must confess, it rained almost every day last summer. But it was enchanting, all the same."

"I don't wonder you find the change to New York exhilarating."

"That's just what I complain of. I'm too much exhilarated. I'm tired of a champagne diet. Besides, everything is brand new. The houses smell of furniture polish. I want to rest my eyes on something belonging to the past."

They had now turned into a broad boulevard, and followed it to an end, indicated by the presence of workmen with their impedimenta making a barrier across the road.

"Let us go on," Carry urged. "Yonder, on that hill-top, I see a genuine old house—one that must have been there since the Revolution at least. I am determined to ride up and have a peep at it."

Apparently uninhabited, but with a sparse curl of smoke issuing from the kitchen chimney, the old house stood in melancholy isolation upon a bluff overlooking the river. The avenue in process of construction beneath it had ruthlessly shaved off the near side of the hill, leaving exposed a steep and gravelly incline crowned with the straggling grasses of an unkempt lawn. Around the white columns of the portico grew walnut and chestnut trees, and in the garden at the rear were seen a ruined summer-house and broken statues arising amid an unpruned growth of box. Cocking their ears cautiously at the unusualness of the proceeding, the horses consented to be guided up a precipitous path along the edge of the acclivity. Barclay was conscious of a feeling of relief when his adventurous young comrade had finally attained her wish, and stood facing the moss-grown portico.

"Nobody lives here, that's plain," said wilful Caroline. "Mr. Barclay, I don't know what you mean to do, but I am determined to explore."

So saying, she slipped lightly from the saddle, gathered up her jaunty habit, and ran around through the weedy garden at the side. Barclay, consigning his horse also to the groom, followed to see her engaged in active conversation with a deaf old dame who emerged from a mouldy kitchen at the rear.

"She says we can get water from the well, and have leave to look at this lovely river view," cried the explorer. "It appears the house is owned by an old maiden lady, whose family has always lived here. If I may trust to my hitherto infallible powers of intuition, the mistress, like the house, is a little out of repair in her upper story, and the maid is afraid of her. Come, Mr. Barclay, grind away at this handle. How long is it since I have had the satisfaction of drinking from the 'moss-covered bucket that hangs in the well?' There, that's deliciously cold and pure. Do you see, this garden must have been a stately one in its prime? I wonder if the ancient dragon could be induced to let us have a glimpse of the interior of the house? I'm positively wild to try."

Nobody withstood Caroline, so Barclay was not particularly surprised to see her return from a second interview with the old woman, beckoning him with a mysterious forefinger.

"We're to see the ground-floor. It is the hour for Miss Stillman's afternoon nap, when she never comes down-stairs. Hush! tread like a burglar, and follow me."

In the wake of the stolid guardian our two young people went from one room to another, filled with handsome furniture of the patterns peculiar to a century ago. Fluted fire-boards, stiff chairs, convex mirrors, black-framed mezzotints, knobs of brass or crystal, held their own, their sway undisputed by the appendages of modern luxury as seen everywhere to-day. It was in the best parlor that their guide came to a halt, waving her withered hand with a faint show of pride in its faded splendor.

"That's all there is to it," she said, in a croaking voice. "I guess them things is solid."

"Either I am dreaming or that portrait of the lady in the red frock with balloon sleeves resembles *you*," Caroline suddenly exclaimed, turning upon Barclay an astonished gaze. "She is enough like you to be your—what?" She paused, puzzled by the date.

"My great-grandmother, great aunt—what you will," said Barclay, laughing. "I wish I were lucky enough to be able to lay claim to her, but, unfortunately, if we have any ancestral respectabilities of this kind in the East, I have yet to be informed of it. My mother, who died in my childhood, was born in the West, and my father is a Westerner, root and branch."

"The likeness is astonishing," pursued Caroline; and even the purblind eyes of the old woman lighted with something like assent.

"*She* 'ain't no one belongin' to her I ever heerd of," went on the old creature, pointing upward with her thumb. "The last on 'em to die was Miss Tabitha, and *she's* Miss Loïs. They was great folks once, I've heerd tell, but that was before I came here. *She* was pinchin' poor till the city tuk the place to run a road through, an' now they say there's a fortin in the bank for her. She don't spend none of it, sartin sure. The two of us don't eat more'n'd keep a mouse from starvin', an' there ain't nobody else."

"I breathe freer," Caroline said, when, after presenting a gratuity to their guide, the two mounted again and rode out of the enclosure. "After all, I like the sunshine best. But I wish I had seen the queer old lady; and as to that portrait, it was simply your double, deny it as you may."

"I am more occupied in wondering if I can get

my horse by that steam-drill down yonder," Edgar said. "He has a rooted objection to anything of the kind, and this path does not offer much room for antics on his part. Your gray is quiet, Miss Heath; you had better wait here, and let me lead the way."

Hardly had he spoken when the engine beneath them sent forth a sudden rush of hissing steam. Caroline repressed an exclamation of alarm. Barclay's horse, rearing violently, grazed the edge of the steep declivity, then set off at a run. Half-way to the bottom he slipped, his rider falling over his head, the horse rolling completely over, and recovering himself to stand shivering with terror beside Barclay's prostrate form. Before a number of men from the gang at work below could reach him Caroline was at his side, the groom following. Barclay, catching one glimpse of her agonized face, bent over him, tried to speak reassuringly, but fainted in the effort. Without consulting the young lady, the men ran up to the house upon the hill, returning with a shutter, upon which they carried the injured man gently along the path he had just descended, laying him down without interference from its guardian in the dim old parlor immediately beneath the portrait of the lady with the balloon sleeves. The bustle of their entrance stirred from her solitude up-stairs the other dweller in this silent mansion. Gliding down like a wraith came a tall woman, with melancholy eyes and chill lips that seemingly had never known a smile.

"Open the window and give him air," cried Caroline, unheeding the approach of the mistress of the house.

"Who gives orders for me?" she said, in a monotonous voice. "It is years since those front windows have been opened."

"It is a matter of life and death," answered the girl, imperiously; and without further opposition the stiff blinds were thrown back, letting in a flood of afternoon sunlight that flowed in a golden stream across the sufferer's temporary couch. Barclay's face thus revealed to view, was untouched by wound or stain. He seemed quietly asleep.

"If a doctor would only come!" began Caroline, interlacing her cold hands. There was an interruption to the quiet of the room, a strange sound, half sob, half laughter, coming from the mistress of the house. Caroline looked up to see the old woman kneeling at Barclay's side, her dull eyes kindled into a sudden rapture of recognition.

"It is Margaret's child. I knew I should see one of them before I die. Oh, my poor wronged sister! After so many years! Thank God! thank God!"

"You'd better coax the old lady to go up-stairs again," said one of the workmen to the servant, touching his forehead significantly. It was evident that all present agreed in his estimate of her mental equilibrium. But until the arrival of a doctor from the neighborhood the gray old woman held the unconscious sufferer's hand in hers, from time to time fondling it against her cheek, and crooning over it words of tenderness. When the surgeon came Caroline, passing an arm around her shoulders, led Miss Loïs from the room.

An hour later Edgar's father and step-mother answered the summons sent them by telephone in the neighborhood, arriving to swell the anxious little group waiting in the dusky hall outside the sick-room. Edgar had returned to consciousness, but the injury to his leg was exquisitely painful, requiring nicest treatment. Until the arrival of Mr. Barclay's family physician, the doctor in charge refused to take the responsibility of sanctioning the removal of his patient. The distressed father walked to and fro in moody silence, and, when twilight brought Dr. Gray, urged him to say that Edgar might be carried in an ambulance to his home.

"On no account," said the doctor. "I can't imagine anything more foolish. Unless these people positively turn you out, he should stay here. His situation is extremely critical. I cannot answer for the consequences of change."

"Here, in this old rattle-trap, with a mad woman for a keeper?" the impatient father wanted to say, but he substituted for it the milder suggestion that they had no claim upon the owner of the house.

"The child of Margaret Lothrop has every claim upon his great-aunt," said the same hollow voice that had startled all a little while before. At his elbow stood Miss Loïs Stillman, holding in her hand a faded daguerrotype at which Mr. Barclay glanced, astonished.

"This!" he exclaimed, looking from it to her again—"This picture my poor wife had taken long ago, to send east at her mother's dying request to Mrs. Lothrop's sisters, who had cast her off for marrying to suit herself. But she never heard from them. They never softened. They let their niece die as they had let her mother, without a token of forgiveness. If you, madam, are, as I suppose, one of those Miss Stillmans, you will understand that I have a reason the more for removing my unfortunate boy from the shelter of *your* roof."

"Oh, have pity!" cried the old woman, pleadingly. "Don't force me to bring charges against the dead. It was Tabitha's will. Tabitha always had her way with me. I—loved—poor—Margaret—dearly. Don't take her grandson from me now."

And thus it was that, by a strange guidance of fate's leading-strings, Margaret Lothrop's grandson was brought into intimate relation with his sole surviving relative upon his mother's side—one who through half a century of alienation and of silence had brooded over the image of her best-loved sister with ever-increasing intensity. Between the handsome lad who for days lay there beneath his grandmother's portrait, uncertain whether death or life would claim him as a prize, and the pallid shade of once beautiful Loïs Stillman, Caroline Heath was the link of warm humanity.

Until the young man's extremity had given place to the joyful promise of convalescence, Carry and her mother, who blamed her child's heedless impetuosity for the accident, made frequent pilgrimages to the hill-top. Then Carry's visits ceased altogether, until one afternoon, when June had clothed the old brown house with roses, she accepted a beseeching invitation from the invalid to have a cup of tea with Aunt Loïs and himself. She found them in the well-remembered parlor, sitting hand in hand, but by-and-by Aunt Loïs arose and stole away. Soon she came back, bearing an antique string of pearls.

"These were intended for our Margaret when she went away to be married against our will," the old lady said, solemnly. "Through poverty and sorrow I have kept them, hoping that some day one of Margaret's granddaughters would come back to receive them at my hands. Now that Edgar is to have all the rest, I want Caroline to wear them as a token of my love and gratitude."

"You are giving them to Margaret's granddaughter, after all, Aunt Loïs," the young man said, triumphantly. And then for the first time in many a long year, tears came into Miss Stillman's eyes, but they were tears of happiness.

THE END.

www.ingramcontent.com/pod-product-compliance
Lightning Source LLC
Chambersburg PA
CBHW020906230426
43666CB00008B/1330